Patterns of Power and Authority
in English Education

Patterns of Power and Authority in English Education

FRANK MUSGROVE
Sarah Fielden Professor of Education
University of Manchester

METHUEN & CO LTD
11 NEW FETTER LANE LONDON EC4

First published in 1971 by Methuen & Co. Ltd.
11 New Fetter Lane London EC4
© 1971 Frank Musgrove
Printed in Great Britain by Butler & Tanner Ltd
Frome and London

SBN 416 16550 8 hardback
SBN 416 16560 5 paperback

This book is available in both hardback and paperback editions. The paperback edition is sold subject to the condition that it shall not, by way of trade or otherwise, be lent, re-sold, hired out, or otherwise circulated without the publisher's prior consent in any form of binding or cover other than that in which it is published and without a similar condition being imposed on the subsequent purchaser.

Distributed in the U.S.A.
by Barnes & Noble Inc

Contents

1	Power, authority and educational goals	*page* 1
2	Impotent schools	13
3	Power, gifts and investment in education	29
4	Humour, sex and power	46
5	Power and the shape and size of schools	55
6	Participation and communication	68
7	The advantages of bureaucracy	88
8	The good headteacher	106
9	The power environment	120
10	Power, the future and the counter-culture	146
	Notes	153
	Index	179

1 Power, authority and educational goals

This book is rooted in the author's ten years of schoolteaching. It is not anecdotal or autobiographical; but the arguments about the nature of power and authority in schools stem principally from this personal experience and make sense to the author in the light of it. If the book has authority, it does not derive from any research that the author has conducted, unless living with and through the problems discussed, throughout a decade, counts as research. If it has power as well as authority, the source is different: it lies in the structure of argument and cogency in presenting a case. It is polemical; it takes sides. In short, the author knows what he thinks about the issues involved. But both the power and the authority of the book are to be judged by teachers against their own practical experience. This, rather than any body of sociological fact or theory, is its measure.

The theme of this book is that schools are underpowered in relation to the goals they try to attain. At the prosaic level of the hour-to-hour performance of their duties, teachers feel that this is so when they complain that they are given authority without the the necessary power to back it up. The distinction between power and authority presents an unending problem to sociologists; in a more pragmatic way it is a never-ending problem for teachers.

The distinction between power and authority that teachers imply is unfamiliar to sociologists. Teachers see their authority as the legitimate demands they can make on pupils by virtue of their office: to be quiet and pay attention, to be punctual and orderly, to perform the tasks they are set in the manner prescribed. They see power as something separate and additional which is also given to them by the system – a tool which enables them to enforce their commands. Since he is not given power which he feels is commensurate with his authority, the teacher may be tempted to exercise power which will equal and perhaps exceed it. Teachers are perpetually poised on the brink of action which is *ultra vires*. In the simplest terms, this means they are tempted to give corporal punishment when they have no authority to do so; and with the knowledge that if pupils refuse to submit, their authority without power is made manifest – and ridiculous. The teacher's problem is that his power falls short of his authority, and so authority itself is in danger of being discredited. The discrepancy between power and authority, as teachers understand these terms, is so great that most teachers live in a state of constant crisis and chronic apprehension. Men and women in other walks of life who were expected to exercise so much authority with so little power would find the job intolerable.

It is true, as Peters says, that a teacher is 'an authority' as well as 'in authority'; and this is an adventitious addition to his power, provided his pupils have some respect for learning, or at least his particular branch of it. But he has less power from adventitious circumstances of this kind than many professional men, who meet their clients only in their hour of greatest need. Although the teacher lives constantly with crisis, it is his crisis: the plumber, the lawyer and the doctor are powerful men who deal with other people's crises: their expertise solves problems of compelling urgency. The infirmities that a teacher's expertise corrects have no such overwhelming immediacy.

Peters sharply distinguishes authority and power, maintaining that they are concepts which 'belong to different families'; but he sees one as alternative to the other in particular circumstances: 'it is only when authority breaks down or when an individual loses his authority that there must be recourse to power if conformity is to be ensured'.[1] On this argument, authority is near to being a form of power, which operates effectively when everyone concerned is prepared to recognize it. Power is in reserve, ready and waiting to do the same job if this recognition is denied.

Sociologists' discussions of power and authority invariably start, and commonly end, with a commentary on what Max Weber said. *Herrschaft* and *Macht* are subjected to intensive scrutiny for their every nuance. Weber, it is often said, defined authority as legitimate power. This is an over-simplification. He made an important distinction between the breadth of power and the specificity of authority. A man's power was not defined or circumscribed by bureaucratic office; but his authority rested on his particular position in an organization's chain of command. Power is personal, authority is social.

Dahrendorf argues: 'The important difference between power and authority consists in the fact that whereas power is essentially tied to the personality of individuals, authority is always associated with social positions or roles.'[2] Authority rests on agreement that an office has particular powers attached to it; power exists regardless of agreement (although Talcott Parsons[3] and 'consensus sociologists' would not recognize this): it is 'merely a factual relationship'.

On this view power and authority have different sources; and when we consider a particular person in an organization, his (personal) power and his (social) authority may be widely discrepant. His power is out of line with his powers. A teacher, by virtue of his qualities of intellect, skill and personality, may have a power in the school far greater than his position as an assistant master without even a graded post would indicate. Having different origins, power and authority can vary independently of each other, and Elliott Jaques has pointed out, in his studies of factory organization, that this can lead to an explosive situation: 'It is an essential of sound organization that power and authority must not be too disparate.'[4] This is as true of schools as it is of factories. Authority adds to power by legitimizing it and mobilizing it to organizational ends. Schools probably have a great deal of unmobilized power which simply seeps away or is actually obstructive. They need more positions of real authority, with genuine powers attached (as distinct from a meaningless multiplication of status labels).

Power and authority interact to a greater extent than is suggested by those who are concerned to distinguish between them; and one of the difficulties of discussing this complex interaction is the poverty of the vocabulary available for the purpose. We need more words.

Rights are themselves a form of power,[5] they are by definition legitimate, and they arise from the social structure. There is also personal power, which arises outside the social structure. The actual power$_1$ of a man's rights, e.g. as a teacher, will depend on his personal power$_2$ to make use of them. Simply to give teachers more rights (power$_1$) will not automatically produce more powerful schools: there is also a problem of recruitment, of bringing powerful men into the profession who can make full use of their formal authority. The 'action approach' to power and authority, which takes into account the characteristics of persons as well as the organization in which they work, is central to this book and is emphasized especially in the penultimate chapter.

The authority of an office, says Dahrendorf, is 'independent of the specific person occupying the position . . .'[6] This, too, is a half-truth. The power of Arnold and of Victoria increased the authority of headship and kingship respectively. A succession of weak men as prime ministers, headmasters or archbishops will diminish the authority of these offices. And for this long-term reason, too, as well as for the short-term enactment of their role, it is important that schools recruit men and women of stature, who would command attention and respect regardless of their particular office.

Throughout this book problems of power and authority are discussed in terms of schools considered as 'bureaucracies'; and investigations of industrial bureaucracies are utilized extensively to throw light on the nature and functioning of schools. It is claimed that these organizations belong to the same 'family' and have common characteristics. Some educationists would dispute this; but the progressive bureaucratization of schools over the past century seems indisputable and provides a historical thread which runs through this book. (It is important, in judging the present, to know whether it is more or less like the past. History is essentially a normative study.) Bureaucratization has been a complex and often internally contradictory development; but the fact of generally increased bureaucratization, and of the overall gain that this represents, are major contentions of this book. Insofar as bureaucracy has meant a more standardized educational product, the power of schools in relation to their social environment has been reduced;

but the gain from bureaucracy in the power, dignity and self-respect of teachers has been incalculable. The problem is to develop educational bureaucracies which are flexible and adaptable, but not subservient, to their environment; and which, from the very uncertainty and unpredictability of their product, will enjoy a powerful bargaining position. Schools which are powerful in realizing the potential of their pupils will indeed be characterized by their uncertainty: they will be a perpetual surprise. As Bernstein says: 'It may well be that one of the tests of an educational system is that its outcomes are relatively unpredictable.'[7]

But there is one respect in which schools are unlike classical bureaucracies and more like industrial organizations: their power gradations are not all on the 'plus' side; their authority structures are dichotomous, with staff 'above the line' and pupils below it. Dahrendorf has pointed out the difference between continuous and dichotomous authority in the following terms:

> Bureaucratic organizations differ from industrial organizations in one important point. Whereas the authority structure of industrial organizations ipso facto defines the borderline that divides the two aggregates of those in positions of dominance and those in positions of subjection, and whereas industrial organizations are in this sense dichotomous, bureaucratic organizations typically display continuous gradations of competence and authority and are hierarchical.[8]

The industrial analogy must not be pushed too far; pupils differ in important respects from industrial 'hands': they have some of the characteristics of clients (even of patients). But the parallel is sufficiently close to carry the same likelihood of endemic conflict. 'With dichotomous organizations', says Dahrendorf, 'class conflict is possible; with hierarchial organizations it is not.' The power struggles that occur in schools, colleges and universities between pupils or students and staff have many of the features of a class struggle; and in schools and universities as in industry, 'participation' of those below the line is felt (by the lower-order participants) to be unreal, bogus, a mere papering over the cracks.

Emphasis is placed in this book on schools in their social environment. A school's linkages with society explain the power relations within it. The linkages are many and varied: some are obvious and blatant, pressure groups like Old Boys' Associations and P.T.A.s; others are more subtle. The distribution of power in society probably has a considerable influence on the selection and organization of knowledge in schools; and this selection and organization in turn has important consequences for power relations in the school. It may or may not be the case that more 'integrated' and 'open' curricula reflect a more 'open' society;[9] but there is little doubt that they diminish the power of senior members of staff and invade the autonomy of pupils. With the traditional 'collection curriculum' – a collection of separate subjects organized in well-defined hierarchies – teachers are vertically organized; with the integrated curriculum horizontal relationships become more important. Familiar boundaries are removed; and with the removal of boundaries goes the removal of protection.

> It is also likely that the weakened classification and relaxed framing of knowledge will encourage more of the pupil to be made public: more of his thoughts, feelings, values. In this way more of the pupil is available for control. As a result, the socialization may be more intrusive, more penetrating.[10]

Eccentricity (social and intellectual) of staff and students has been possible within the traditional boundaries of academic subjects – majestic manifestations of power and defiance. When we have all finally been integrated, we shall have only agreement, uniformity, and co-operation left.

Headmasters who wish to reduce their subordinates' power and increase their own will be wise to abolish subjects and integrate the curriculum. For subjects are centres of power. They are also centres of authority. They help to make up the pluralism of power which is a crucial check on the power of headmasters, principals and vice-chancellors. Autocratic heads of schools and colleges will decry subject boundaries and initiate policies of integration and hybridization. They will be in the forefront of the progressives who attack such obvious and easy targets as 'narrow specialization' and the 'compartmentalization of knowledge', and who proclaim (perhaps on the authority of Benjamin Bloom) the natural superiority of synthesis, as opposed to analysis and mere description, in the hierarchy of intellectual operations. They will not attach much weight to classification as the basis of systematic thought and the importance of putting together things that belong together. They will discredit the very concept of a boundary. It is already one of the most disgraceful concepts in education. And in removing boundaries, they will remove important and legitimate defences of those within them. Integrated curricula are powerless curricula, wide open to centralized control. They present no effective curb on the will of the man at the top.

'Subjects' can be regarded as bureaucracies, often with a considerable material endowment (in the form of scholarships, fellowships and various honours), hierarchically controlled, deciding the conditions of membership, staunchly maintaining their boundaries, inventing ideologies, even utopias, to justify their existence.[11] But they are located in a wider world and need its support. They will receive this, says Young, if their values accord with those of the socially powerful. He has pointed out that the Schools Council and similar bodies bent on curriculum innovation have been able to promote change only in the low status, non-academic areas of education in which powerful interests have no stake. Knowledge, he rightly says, is stratified; rather more doubtfully he claims that this stratification is closely linked with social stratification and that 'the criteria of high status knowledge are associated with the values of dominant social groups'.[12] High status knowledge is still literary, abstract and non-applied because dominant social groups received their education in these terms, believe it to be valuable, wish to see it perpetuated and, above all, will recruit to their own ranks only those who have been similarly educated.

This thesis has considerable plausibility, especially when viewed from All Souls (or even from the University of London Institute of Education). But the mechanism whereby this power over the curriculum is exercised by dominant social groups is obscure. There is of course an intricate network of personal interconnectedness which binds Oxford and Cambridge and the higher civil service. Academics in the postwar world have become powerful men sitting on Whitehall committees. Shils has pointed to the strength of the 'London–Oxford–Cambridge Axis',[13] and overlapping power structures in the nation's life have recently been examined in terms of linkages through circulating personnel:

> The academic world, then, seems to be increasingly tied to government not just by the carefully forged links of the University Grants Committee, but by a fine web of involvement through individual careers, advisory services and the organization of research. It is difficult to combine influence in the academic world with the role of the aloof intellectual in society, the value of which was stressed by Karl Mannheim.[14]

It is true that the curriculum values supported in these particular circles are rooted in the aristocratic–gentry culture which Shils sees resurgent in postwar Oxbridge. 'The aristocratic–gentry culture has now come back into the saddle, with little to dispute its dominion.' Scientists in Whitehall remain lowly in status and relatively ill-paid. And even

> scientists turned administrators have shown no particular desire to improve the lot of their scientific employees. It is clear that any move to improve the status of scientists in government employment would have to be radical indeed in order to alter the patterns which have been consecrated by tradition and supported by prejudice.[15]

It would be dangerous to generalize from the parochial world of Oxford, Cambridge and the higher civil service to the wider national life. Shils himself drew a very sharp distinction between the curricular values of Oxford (which do not, in fact, stress specialization, and give grudging support to research) and those of the great provincial universities (which *are* specialized, research-oriented – and even 'applied'). Indeed, the really effective technological universities are not the post-Robbins creations but the major civic universities with deep roots in the bourgeois culture of the Victorian past.

The mechanism by which 'dominant social groups' are alleged to stratify knowledge has quite failed to operate with respect to the new technological universities; and the reason must be sought not in the wider social structure, but in local institutional circumstances. The notion that a curriculum which is literary, abstract and non-applied carries high status would be remarkable to any lecturer in humanities or social studies in a new technological university. From Cambridge

Ashby could claim with confidence for the entire universe of higher learning that technology was tolerated in universities but not assimilated. 'It is not yet taken for granted that a faculty of technology enriches a university intellectually as well as materially.'[16] Writing in the nineteen-fifties, Ashby was without foreknowledge of the power structure of the transfigured C.A.T.s.

Subservient to departments of science, technology and engineering, the humanities and social sciences in the new technological universities have no illusions about their status in the curriculum. Service departments before university status was granted, they remain service departments slightly disguised. They may gain a measure of self-determination by treaty, on strictly contract terms, for their services to departments of technology. The idea that teachers and students in departments of technology are characterized by humility and a proper sense of their lowly position in the world of learning and society at large, dies hard:[17] it finds no support in observation and research.[18] Quite the contrary: their attitudes are arrogant. Staff and students in the humanities and social sciences are held in contempt as people of inferior abilities in soft options – idlers, layabouts and unemployables; their mode of intellectual activity is treated with derision.[19] 'Liberal Studies' are characterized not by freedom and liberality, but by servility.

The link between the power-structure of society and the stratification of knowledge requires close investigation. Another link between schools and society is through their goals. 'Power' is treated in this book primarily in the Parsonian sense of the capacity of persons or collectivities to mobilize resources for the attainment of goals, especially when these goals are obstructed by some kind of human resistance or opposition. The goals in question are the goals of schools as formal organizations, and 'organizations are always sub-systems of larger systems, the goal of one sub-system being a means or input of a different sub-system'.[20] It is through the nature and definition of their goals that schools are vulnerable to, or protected from, the pressures of their social environment.

The sociological literature on organizational goals is now extensive. It warns us that the goals imputed to an organization may be merely the goals of top managers,[21] that organizations do not spend all, or even most, of their efforts on goal attainment,[22] and that the notion of a specific goal as the origin and cause of an organization is an unhistorical myth.[23] All these warnings have force in relation to schools. The goals of headmasters are not necessarily the goals of others involved in the organization – assistant staff, pupils and parents;[24] a high proportion of a school's efforts are usually devoted to 'support goals' (promoting pride in the school and esprit de corps etc.) rather than 'output goals' ('the character of a good citizen' etc.);[25] and the goals of schools have a way of being succeeded and displaced, earlier ones lost in the mists of antiquity. This is not necessarily, or even commonly, a process of updating. The progression of goals is usually away from direct social applicability. Schools and universities commonly have multiple goals, and a division of labour makes the effective pursuit of disparate goals possible. Single-pattern, integrated curricula with no clear division of labour tend to restrict the range and diversity of goals that a school can pursue.

Goals must be distinguished from social function. Teachers can usually state at least the intrinsic goals of their schools and of their subjects, especially after they have taken their postgraduate certificate in education – although some of the goals may be utopian, often voiced but seldom supported in actual behaviour; and other goals may escape notice or be too obvious for verbalization. But the social function of a subject, a school, or an educational system will be known only to sociologists and historians. Indeed, teachers may strongly deny these functions (e.g. the promotion of social mobility or the immobilization of the economically redundant[26]), even when sociologists bring them to their attention.

Training is predestined to subservience, education to irrelevance. Training is vulnerable, education is protected: the former is widely exposed to environmental pressures, the latter is insulated. Schools and universities learn to protect themselves from the social environment by emphasizing their intrinsic rather than their extrinsic goals; the development of their autonomy is largely the story of substituting intrinsic goals (which are in theory unwilled, arising naturally and inevitably out of an activity) for extrinsic (which are superimposed, conceptually distinct, defined by society). Training institutions, which have overwhelmingly extrinsic goals, are the creatures of their environment. Institutions which offer education rather than training attenuate their links with society and abate its pressures. Few organizations can totally disavow output goals and actually gain in importance by doing so – as schools may do when they proclaim learning for its own sake. (Defence for its own sake is on show at the Tower of London.) The development of subject ideologies and utopias is largely a process of inventing intrinsic goals for activities which were in origin instrumental and applied. Even physical education and domestic science have discovered such philosophies. Classical studies have probably had the most remarkable succession of goals since the days when they were the key to the natural sciences: every new goal has been more intrinsic than the last, except when they were pressed into proconsular service at Jowett's Balliol.

Total irrelevance is a position as powerless as total subservience. The problem of the autonomous is still to be needed. It is often solved by educational institutions not through their formal offerings, but through informal adjustments and response to social needs. Schools and universities respond to their social environments informally and unofficially (and therefore less dangerously) not through the curriculum, but through the extra-curriculum. Vocational technical colleges with overburdened timetables which leave time for nothing else, are in danger of being far less socially responsive than the Classical Sixth. Technology has blossomed in the schools as an extra-curricular activity (most publicized at Sevenoaks).[27] The Oxford Union, rather than P.P.E., trains future prime ministers; the Cambridge Footlights, rather than the English Tripos, trains television satirists. The extra-curriculum is as serious, utilitarian and instrumental as children's play in a primitive society.[28]

A flexible extra-curriculum makes possible the dissociation of curricular and organizational goals. In Victorian public schools modern languages, science, and even mathematics at Eton under Stephen Hawtrey, had a thriving extra-curricular existence before they were formally incorporated. In a similar fashion applied mathematics developed at Oxford and Cambridge in the sixteenth and seventeenth centuries outside the formal curriculum:

> Hakluyt found in Oxford a group of men already interested in the new mathematics, astronomy, map-making etc. In Cambridge

at the turn of the century a galaxy of mathematicians is found, centred mainly on Gonville and Caius, Trinity, King's and Emmanuel Colleges. The point has been made, however, that much of this new learning was pursued in extra-statutory channels. The formal structure of the curriculum was only slowly modified.[29]

It is partly through this informal adjustment to social needs that the main curriculum purchases its autonomy. The problem of schools and universities is to achieve autonomy without losing their bargaining power. The status of educational institutions is less a function of the curriculum than the extra-curriculum: schools and colleges which have no such penumbra of activities are generally low in esteem. Informal education is a neglected factor in the equation of power.

2 Impotent schools

Schools are underpowered in relation to the goals they try to attain. (In relation to the more ambitious societal goals which they are commonly set by politicians and the public – world peace, interracial harmony, the elimination of crime and economic abundance – they are chronically underpowered.) People more directly involved in schools set more modest and apparently realistic goals: the effective transmission of a body of knowledge, the promotion of physical, intellectual and artistic skills, the inculcation of socio-moral values and attitudes, and the development of acceptable habits of behaviour. Neither teachers as individuals nor the arrangements within which they work are sufficiently powerful for more than modest success in these modest aims. Even the allegedly omnipotent 'total institution', to which some schools approximate, is most remarkable, on close scrutiny, for its ineptitude. The problem of contemporary education is to put more power into the system in order to overcome obstacles and resistances to the attainment of its goals.

It is the argument of this chapter that a general expansion in the power of teachers at all levels of the school hierarchy is necessary for increased effectiveness. This means that more teachers must be able to take final decisions, or have a genuine voice in such decisions, which relate to the circumstances in which they work. In this way the system might even attract more men who are powerful as persons, as well as by virtue of their office. This is the view expressed by Mr Roger Young, headmaster of George Watson's College, Edinburgh, in his Speech Day address, 1970:

At a time of shortage of teachers, what was badly needed was an increase in the powers delegated to them and a devolution of authority from the administrative and political centre to the schools themselves, such that more men and women would be attracted to a way of life offering greater opportunities for responsible decision alongside the satisfactions of working with and for young people.[1]

The power that teachers exercise may be normative, remunerative or coercive. The generally approved form of power in education today is normative, exercised by bringing pupils to share or accept a common value-system (or 'normative structure'). Remunerative power based on the prizes, honours and rewards available to teachers and schools is generally less approved. Superimposed discipline is wholly discreditable. But every experienced and effective teacher uses a judicious admixture of bluff (made necessary by shortage of coercive power), coercion (the exercise of such coercive power as he has), and appeals to his pupils' better nature. Coercive and normative power do not cancel each other out quite as automatically as is sometimes supposed.[2]

Many a teacher lives an unnecessarily miserable – and relatively ineffective – life because he has been taught in training that normative control is not only right but sufficient. The conjunction of human-relations social psychology, normative-consensus sociology, and reward-reinforcement psychology in the second quarter of the twentieth century has made the teacher's task doubly difficult. Societies hang together as going and effective concerns with varying combinations of normative and coercive power. As Wright Mills has observed: 'Even in such sacred little groups as families, the unity of "common values" is by no means necessary: distrust and hatred may be the very stuff needed to hold a loving family together.'[3] And at the heart of a teacher's power (whether normative or coercive) is his involvement in decisions about the arrangements within which he works: 'insofar as such decisions are made (and insofar as they could be but are not) the problem of who is involved in making them (or not making them) is the basic problem of power'.[4]

Pitfalls abound in the study of goal-attainment in education. The problems of goal-definition – and, indeed, of goal detection – were discussed in chapter one; the technical problems of estimating or measuring their attainment are as difficult. There is the familiar problem of quantifying intangible goals, and the danger of regarding as important and legitimate only those goals that can easily be quantified. The fragmentary and admittedly imperfect evidence that we have suggests that even the ostensible and commonsense goals of educational organizations are infrequently attained; and that when they are, the explanation is often to be found in other circumstances than the efforts of the school. Factors such as the abilities of pupils, and the often-demonstrated influence of parental attitudes, set limits to what can be achieved. Some American research into the power of universities to change their students between entry and graduation has produced profoundly pessimistic results. The characteristics of the 'input' determined the characteristics of the 'output' four years later. This was the conclusion from a follow-up study of students who, in 1961, entered thirty-eight universities with widely differing provisions and variations in 'environmental quality' (including the qualifications of academic staff). 'Institutional quality' appeared to have no effect on the final product: 'differences in student achievement during the senior year were much more highly dependent upon variations in student characteristics that existed before entrance into college than upon the characteristics of the undergraduate college attended'.[5]

These conclusions relate to readily measurable levels of scholastic performance. Studies of English primary schools in these terms are less disheartening. Douglas's information on the progress of a national sample of children between the age of eight and eleven showed how great was the influence of parental interest; but the best and the worst schools entirely nullified the effects of parents' attitudes. In primary schools with a good academic record, even children whose parents were uninterested in their progress obtained the number of grammar school places that could be expected on the basis of their attainments at eight years of age.[6] Unfortunately Douglas had no information about the special characteristics of these potent schools apart from the somewhat tautological statement that they had a history of potency.

The Plowden Report on *Children in their Primary Schools* attempted to estimate the relative contribution of various relevant circumstances to scholastic attainment (as measured by a test of reading comprehension). Again, parental attitudes made the major contribution to within-school and between-school differences: 'The most striking feature of both these sets of comparisons is the large part played by parental attitudes . . .'[7] The 'state of the school', which covered facts about school organization and the experience, qualifications and competence of teachers as judged by head-teachers and H.M.I.s, was relatively unimportant. Wiseman reached a similar conclusion after his extensive and sophisticated inquiries into the functioning of schools in their social environments:

> The statement that educational attainment depends upon school conditions seems to most people a statement of the obvious. And yet we know surprisingly little about *what* school conditions are the most important in this respect. It will be clear . . . that the argument being developed here is that factors of attitude and motivation are more important – in the secondary school particularly – than the more obvious physical factors such as quality of building, size of class, etc., and more important than even the quality of teaching, if this is used in the narrow sense of teaching technique and instructional method.[8]

The grammar school has traditional objectives, which are well established, clearly defined and generally understood with respect to both academic attainment and personal development;[9] and it has organized itself to attain these goals. In terms of academic attainment its success, as testified by the Ministry's *Early Leaving* report of 1954, is not spectacular: 38 per cent of its pupils either failed to stay the O-level course or passed in no more than two subjects. It is true that the grammar school is reluctant to be judged in terms of examination failure or success; but even in the area of 'character development', recent research suggests that its effectiveness may be no greater.

King's study of value-changes among a grammar school's pupils is a study of educational disaster. All the indications were that pride in school and moral character deteriorated over the five-year O-level course. If staff had values with 'a heavy middle class loading', they signally failed to shift the load on to their pupils. Teachers attached the highest importance to inculcating moral values: the practice of honesty and truthfulness, the belief that there is more to life than material gratification, and tolerance. They approved of their pupils' theatre-going, listening to classical music, joining the Boy Scouts; they disapproved of their listening to pop records, playing solo and ten-pin bowling. They approved of their playing bridge. 'It can be assumed that the teachers must have made some conscious effort to transmit these values to their pupils'. Their failure was total. During their grammar school careers pupils declined in their respect for honesty and truthfulness; they placed less emphasis on wanting employment in which they could be helpful to others; they read less widely; they showed no inclination to choose more interests and activities approved by the school; and they showed no tendency to become more tolerant.[10]

One reason why schools are impotent is that they are a bore. (Few curricula can compete with a kestrel.) This is no more than one would expect of schools which, as was pointed out in chapter one, are performing their classical tasks in a radically transformed social environment: no longer information-poor but information-rich, no longer action-rich but action-poor. The Schools' Council inquiry into attitudes to school among a national sample of school leavers showed that a majority were oppressed by the monotony of school: 55 per cent of the 15-year-old boys and 58 per cent of the girls agreed that 'School is the same day after day, week after week'.[11] One broad category of answers about the advantages of being at work compared with school 'related to the greater interest and variety that a job offered: "I'll be doing something different every day"; "Different things happening"; "If you do a job and finish it you'll start another one next week"; "We won't have all that boring talk".'[12]

Yet there are schools which are too potent, which consistently produce 'over-achievers'. Potency in academic matters must refer to the effective production of intellectually autonomous people, who will function well in other settings, without the support of a particular school structure. The concept of achievement is a difficult one; still more difficult are the concepts of under- and over-achievement. There is the logical difficulty of conceiving someone achieving more than he is capable of: but there is less difficulty in conceiving someone who will perform intellectual tasks well under particular circumstances of exhortation and careful preparation.

The characteristics of the over-potent school are no better established than those of a merely potent school. (The two are often confused, when in practice they are probably antithetical.) Over-potency probably accounts for the poor predictive value of A-level results for university work that some (but by no means all) investigators have found. A-level results will be predictive if they are obtained in a merely potent school. Wankowski found at the University of Birmingham that A-level results were comparatively poor predictors in the case of students from independent, direct-grant and grammar schools; they were good predictors in the case of students from relatively unselective and comprehensive schools. (The difference was particularly pronounced for males.) Wankowski makes the assumption that the non-selective schools are less 'pressurized', less coercive both socially and scholastically.[13] Attainments reflect the quality of pupils, and not the characteristics of the schools.

The teacher is a classroom manager who takes decisions about goals to be pursued and the means of attaining them. The over-powerful teacher is perhaps the one who takes all the decisions and leaves nothing to the discretion of pupils. The merely powerful teacher may set goals and give directions for getting there, or he may not. He may exercise his power by not taking the decisions that he might have done. The powerful teacher may be the 'autocratic' teacher of the research literature; equally he may be the 'democratic' teacher. But he is not the laissez-faire teacher.[14] It is the laissez-faire teacher who is the powerless teacher: he takes no decisions, not from deliberate choice, but because no one would take any notice if he did.

The total power available to a teacher in the classroom is the sum of his power as a person, the power he derives from the authority of his office, and the power he derives from the authority of his subject. The first and last are the most variable. Subjects vary considerably in their authoritativeness, the respect they command, the cogency of their case to be taught at all. In the general population of 15-year-old school leavers, the humanities (defined as current affairs, geography, history and religious instruction) carry little weight on various counts.[15] A weak teacher will gain greatly in power, even in a secondary modern school, from teaching mathematics; only a powerful man should venture to teach scripture anywhere. (There is a tendency for science subjects, with a large body of incontrovertible fact, to be 'authoritarian' and to attract 'authoritarian' teachers – but this is a different issue.) The authority of subjects for pupils rests on extrinsic as well as intrinsic considerations: they are authorized for many by vocational relevance.[16] All non-examination subjects are de-authorized. A teacher of non-examinable liberal studies in a technological university must be as strong a man as someone in a secondary modern school taking R.I.

The debate about the consequences of using power to make decisions or not to make decisions: to be 'authoritarian' or 'democratic', is still open. The evidence is conflicting and bedevilled by the variety of definitions not only of authoritarian-democratic teacher-behaviour, but of the 'achievement' to which it leads or fails to lead. On balance teacher- rather than pupil-decision-taking seems to lead to greater productivity of learning as conventionally measured. One of the first apparent vindications of authoritarian teaching, published by Brookover in 1943, was based on what were virtually rote-memory tests in History.[17] Whether it leads as efficiently to other educational outcomes such as creativity (even as conventionally measured) and the promotion of higher-order cognitive skills (such as 'critical thinking') is more doubtful. Democratic or pupil-centred teaching has often been shown to be no more effective than teacher-centred teaching as measured by orthodox examination procedures; but it may be the case that it has desirable educational consequences which the techniques available to us cannot measure.[18]

Decision-taking parents seem to produce good material for the school system (or at least, for the American high school system). Mothers of high-achieving American pupils think that children should make only minor decisions for themselves and should accept parental decisions regarding choice of occupation, religion and friends. '... it was found that the mothers of high achievers were more authoritarian and restrictive in the treatment of their children than the mothers of low achievers.' 'Thus it would appear that the high achiever is a child who has a rigidly defined place within the home which he is expected to keep with docile acceptance.'[19]

There are periodical reviews of research into 'progressive' teaching methods, with tallies of pro-democratic and pro-authoritarian results. One survey of thirty-two inquiries concluded: '... 11 studies have reported greater learning from learner-centred groups, 13 have shown no difference, and 8 have found teacher-centred methods superior ... '[20] Much depends on the precise form of attainment in question. Many forms of attainment are doubtless encouraged by authoritarian parents reinforced by authoritarian teachers. What progressive, pupil-centred situations are most likely to foster is high morale (or 'group cohesiveness', or simply happiness); although this is less likely in groups with a task, as distinct from a social-emotional, goal.[21] Common assumptions about the connection between morale and productivity are called into question by research in this area: high productivity is not a consequence of high morale, but an alternative. At most the relationship is probably curvilinear; if morale and therefore social cohesion are too low, the communication necessary for efficiency does not occur; if it is too high, difficult tasks, which might put everyone under strain, are not attempted for fear of destroying it. People who need to apply themselves to tasks which are not invariably exciting, and have few immediate intrinsic or extrinsic rewards, may need to be constrained; and they may not be particularly happy. When tasks of this kind need to be done, the powerful teacher will insist that they are – even at the risk of disrupting the good relationships he has built up. Good relationships may be a serious impediment to educational attainment. From time to time the effective teacher may have to insist that something actually be done.

Both democratic and authoritarian teaching and learning are expressions of the teacher's power. Powerlessness is found in the laissez-faire conditions of drift which Hargreaves found at Lumley Secondary Modern School. Such circumstances may have the appearance of 'progressiveness': reduced social distance between teachers and taught, and general informality and good fellowship. But to try actually to do anything was to threaten the prevailing harmony; and nobody tried. Peace rested on clearly understood treaty obligations and 'Life was directed towards a reduction of potential conflict by a minimal imposition of demands upon one another.'[22]

The powerful teacher will promote teacher-centred or pupil-centred learning according to the outcome he wants. Pupil-centred, progressive methods seem – on Warburton's evidence – to be conducive to attainment, among secondary modern school pupils, in reading ability (but not in arithmetic).[23] They may also be associated in the primary school with high scores on tests of divergent thinking[24] – although Hudson places considerable stress on the value of unhappiness.[25] It is probable that most of the intellectual skills and accomplishments deemed necessary at the secondary stage of education, and assessed by traditional examinations, are best promoted by teacher-centred teaching. But whether the teaching mode adopted is 'democratic' or 'authoritarian', it is likely to be effective if it is the expression of the teacher's power to decide. And one way to increase the power of the teacher in his classroom is to have all the subjects he teaches examined for certificates; and ruthlessly to prune the curriculum of those extensive areas which have entirely lost their credibility.

The power of all the provisions and arrangements which go to make up the life of a school is commonly directed to promoting change in outlook and behaviour as well as in knowledge and intellectual ability. Power in these respects is said to rest on a school's 'pervasiveness' – the range of activities both within and outside the school for which it sets standards and has clear expectations; and especially on its 'scope' – the number of different activities in which members are jointly involved. Etzioni maintains that: 'High scope enhances normative control. . . . All other things being equal, residential colleges can have a considerably deeper impact, with the same investment of normative control.'[26] 'Total institutions', as described by Goffman, are wide in scope (though they may be low in pervasiveness); and Goffman has claimed that: 'In our society, they are the forcing houses for changing persons.'[27] What is in fact remarkable about the total institutions that have been studied – including the asylum investigated by Goffman himself – is their general failure to change anyone very much.

This does not undermine a widespread faith in their potency and the sanctity of the residential principle; although the Newcastle Commission of 1861 recommended Day Training Colleges on the ground that the residential college was too wide in 'scope' and promoted little but timidity:

> Students in a training school are, considering their age and circumstance, too gregarious; they live too much in a mass. They study together, they take all their meals together, they occupy a common room in the intervals of recreation, they have no privacy, they are scarcely ever alone except when in bed. Hence there is little opportunity for self-recollection or private meditation. . . .[28]

This is the very batch existence that Goffman saw as the hallmark of a total institution:

> First, all aspects of life are conducted in the same place and under the same single authority. Second, each phase of the members' daily activity is carried on in the immediate company of a large batch of others, all of whom are treated alike and required to do the same thing together. Third, all phases of the day's activities are tightly scheduled, with one activity leading at a prearranged time into the next, the whole sequence of activities being imposed from above by a system of explicit formal rules and a body of officials.[29]

This has every appearance of a blue-print for organizational potency. Goffman's account of an asylum is in fact an anatomy of impotence.

This abnormally 'encompassing'[30] establishment fails to encompass. Goffman's inmate is busy making 'secondary adjustments', he is refusing to become a 'normal', 'programmed', built-in member; he uses unauthorized means, or ends, or both, 'thus getting around the organization's assumptions as to what he should do and get and hence what he should be'.[31] He dodges the impact of his organizational environment through one or more modes of adaptation. He may simply withdraw, become apathetic, show a 'drastic curtailment in interactional events';[32] he may show intransigence, flagrant refusal to co-operate with staff; he may become a colonizer, making life as cosy as possible in his particular corner;

and he may adapt through 'conversion', enacting a hypocritical role as the perfect inmate. He may adopt all these modes at different times, according to circumstances; but in any event he has evaded the pressures of the institution and refused to be modified by them.

It has become fashionable to examine English public schools as total institutions; and in the process the concept of 'totality' has been subjected to overdue critical scrutiny. Lambert has maintained that a distinction should be made between expressive and instrumental totality: 'the concept of totality can imply either a physical or a normative component or both'.[33] This appears to correspond to the distinction drawn earlier between 'scope' and 'pervasiveness'. Goffman's total institution is low in pervasiveness (normative totality), wide in scope (physical totality). English public schools are much higher in pervasiveness and much narrower in scope than the establishments which Goffman regarded as total.

They differ, too, in other important respects, as Wakeford has pointed out. Public schoolboys engage in relatively few activities in unison (they do not have such a literal batch existence as Goffman's inmates); and they are not 'like-situated' – they are ordered in a well-defined status hierarchy. Nevertheless, Wakeford considers the parallel with total institutions to be worth making, and the concept to be worth using in his study of an English public school.

And like Goffman's book on asylums, Wakeford's book on the 'cloistered élite' is a study of the failure of power to be powerful. Yet the public school does not normally need to make radical changes in its inmates. Pupils are largely 'pre-socialized', and their 'presenting culture' is scarcely different from the culture of the school. Careful selection procedures ensure that this is so.[34] The indications are that when the presenting culture is different, when the school has to deal with more recalcitrant (e.g. working-class) material, its impact is derisory. This is the picture that emerges from Lambert's observations of 'socially integrated' boarding schools. He points out that in all schools pupils tend to support some official values and to reject others; but 'This is particularly so in integrated schools, where the boys from L.E.A. backgrounds support the academic ends of the school but not so much the wider moral, social or cultural ones.'[35] Local authority scholars tend to reject the aims of the school, but to show a cynical preparedness to go along with the means. Such hypocrisy is to be found in any school, but seems to be especially prevalent in integrated schools, 'where it is a common response to any expressive ends in the school, religious or cultural inculcation. . . . '[36] Even Lambert's 'hothouse society' fails to be the effective forcing-house that his title suggests.

Merton gave us one typology of deviance[37] (Innovation, Ritualism, Retreatism and Rebellion); Goffman gave us another (Withdrawal, Intransigence, Colonization and Conversion). Wakeford has combined the two. Responses to organizational pressures can be described in terms of acceptance or rejection of goals and the means of attaining them. Goals may be accepted whilst means are rejected, and vice versa. Sometimes the response falls short of either outright acceptance or rejection, and is better described as indifference.[38] A public schoolboy's adaptation to his total institution is frequently of this order.

Typically the public schoolboy camps out in the school. He is a colonizer. He establishes a comfortable, even a cosy existence, and settles down to make the best of things 'for the duration'. He makes the most of such minor gratifications as are available. He presents no great challenge to the school; he keeps out of trouble; he maintains at least the appearance of keeping to official rules. Such 'colonization', Wakeford maintains, is the majority adaptation in the first years of school life, and in the last. Only in the third year is there a different majority adaptation – 'intransigence', expressed principally in physical appearance, hair length and clothing styles. There is a prevailing indifference to the goals of the school, and a rejection of means. Two other forms of adaptation – 'retreatism' and 'rebellion' – involve only a minority of pupils. Retreatists are found in the earlier years of school life: they are indifferent to the goals and means of the school, but put nothing in their place. Like tramps in the wider world, they are in society but not of it. Rebels occur typically in the final years at school. They reject ends and means and substitute new ones. They refuse to become prefects, to accept other positions of responsibility, and to have fags. They take up a self-consciously ideological position against all that the school stands for.

The conformists, who accept the school's ends and means, are at any stage a minority. They are likely to be science specialists or boys with good sports records. At least in the eyes of staff (and perhaps of parents), these are the boys with whom the school has been successful. But: 'Contrary to the expectations of many staff and parents, this is not the mode which is adopted by most of the boys for most of their school life.'[39]

Wakeford offers an essentially descriptive account of deviance and conformity in a public school; he makes little attempt to explain the pattern of response that he observed. The very totality of the system, the prison-like circumstances of which boys complained, doubtless provoked resistance and so undermined its power. But what remain entirely hidden are the reasons for the difference in styles and modes of resistance. Age, success in sports and science specialization are the only suggested correlates. Perhaps the study of an organization's power to attain its goals should be conducted in a quite different conceptual framework.

Parsons has argued that power is a circulating medium analogous to money and capable of 'expansion' in much the same way – through the creation of credit. He conceives of a process of power-enhancement which is 'strictly parallel to economic investment'.[40] Power is generated by a social system much as wealth is generated by the productive organization of the economy. The power that Parsons has in mind is 'the capacity to secure performance', 'the capacity of persons or collectivities "to get things done" effectively, in particular when their goals are obstructed by some kind of human resistance or opposition'. He opposes the view that there is a fixed quantity of power in any relational system and that any gain on the part of A must by definition occur by diminishing the power at the disposal of other units, B, C and D. In short, he denies that power is a zero-sum phenomenon.

This thesis has received a good deal of critical attention.[41] In particular, Parsons' apparent failure to distinguish between power and authority has been pointed out: all power, for Parsons, is legitimate; the power expansion that he talks about is an expansion of trust, it is possible because there is agreement among everyone concerned, whether subordinate or superordinate; it is based on consensus. But it is precisely agreement among the members of a 'relational system' that may be at issue – the root of the problem of power.

But the simple pragmatic notion that Parsons is advancing – that A may have more power without B having less – has support in common observation of life, and in the empirical studies of Tannenbaum. One simple and obvious way of giving organizations more power to attain their goals is to give all their members more power – right down the line. Parsons comes near to contradiction when he says that there can be more power if members surrender theirs to one man and put unlimited trust in him. Hobbes, Rousseau, Hitler and Stalin had said it long before. Parsons threw in the democratic safeguard that members could withdraw their investment in their leader if it failed to pay off. Investors would get more power in the long run by surrendering their power now. More logically (and sensibly) everyone can invest more power in everyone else. The powerful organization does not necessarily redistribute power; it totalizes power by increasing it at all levels.

Tannenbaum's first attempt to study the total amount of power in organizations, as well as its distribution, was carried out in voluntary organizations, the local associations of the League of Women Voters in America. Members estimated the amount of power at the disposal of fellow members at different levels in the organization, and power was plotted against hierarchical level.[42] Attempts were made to relate both total power and the distribution of power to organizational morale and organizational effectiveness. In these voluntary associations the clearest relationship was between democratic control and high morale.

A more ambitious study covering two hundred organizational units (mainly work organizations) indicated that while 'democracy' might be important for morale in voluntary organizations,[43] it was generally irrelevant to both morale and effectiveness in work organizations. Lower level members generally wanted more power than they thought they had, but 'they do not view this ideal as lowering the control to be exercised by the managerial supervisors'. Clearly the members of these diverse work organizations did not conceive power as a zero-sum phenomenon. 'The ideal pattern proposed by most members does not often imply radical or dysfunctional aspirations regarding control. On the contrary, it implies a higher degree of total control....' (Similar studies carried out in American schools have produced similar results: 'when teachers perceive their principal's level of influence to be high, they are likely to perceive their own level of influence to be relatively high.'[44])

The crucial relationship established in these investigations was between total power and organizational effectiveness. In the most diverse organizations – delivery company stations, car sales organizations, and a wide range of other enterprises – effectiveness (and often morale) were related to total power. 'Substantial control exercised by both leaders and members appears to be a correlate of high organizational performance in the majority of organizations examined.'

If organizational effectiveness is related to total organizational power, there is a case for exploring the means of 'totalizing' power in schools. An indiscriminate increase in everybody's power would be unlikely to have the desired effect: increases would occur within the existing division of labour. Four heads of the French department would be unlikely to quadruple the French department's power; it might quarter it. If more power positions are created, their areas of competence require definition and delimitation; and if they do not overlap, they must be effectively coordinated. A division of labour in the exercise of power might distinguish between judicial, executive and legislative power: some members of the school would have positions of importance in one area, some in another. In a rather untidy and unsystematic way, universities already provide power positions in these different spheres: Senate has important judicial functions, sitting in judgement not on persons but on schemes and proposals which come up from departmental and faculty levels. Legislative bodies might also specialize, one dealing with academic provisions, another with disciplinary rules. And authority positions should be created whenever a teacher of power emerges for whom there is no functional senior post – analogous to the personal chairs that universities confer. And correlatively non-experts should not be given an expert's powers. One of the surest ways of diminishing the total power of any educational institution, whether school, college or university, is to dilute its authoritative bodies in the name of democracy. An influx of non-authoritative persons into an expert body is the surest way to reduce its authority and hence its power – and to leave the headmaster, principal or vice-chancellor in undisputed command, not through trust (or 'investment'), but by default.

3 Power, gifts and investment in education

Teachers are relatively powerless because they have little to offer that their pupils urgently want. By the same token, even headmasters have power over their staff only within quite circumscribed limits: they have few gifts to offer, apart from approval and perhaps occasional unmerited promotions, with which to place their subordinates under obligation. It is chiefly through their (limited) power, not to apply rules, but to suspend them, that teachers have power over pupils and headmasters over teachers. The power of schools over pupils is probably related to the 'price' they exact from them. If the price they demand of pupils is high, in terms of rigorous entrance standards and relentless effort and even hardship once they are in, schools may have considerable power to modify pupils' behaviour, perhaps especially after they have left. When they have given so much throughout their schooldays, Old Boys will seldom admit that it was not really worth it: in retrospect the experiences of schooldays will acquire a remarkable potency. Guardsmen like Etonians are created in the ten years after their discharge. The power of schools may be long delayed, operating through a process of retroactive socialization.

The theory of social exchange[1] may degenerate into tautology.[2] All social relations involve giving and receiving. 'Social exchange' may be merely synonymous with 'social bond'. But often people are more or less deliberate in the gifts they give or accept: they weigh the likely returns and obligations involved. In these circumstances social exchange may be genuinely manipulative and an important source of power.

Indeed, social exchange is more flexible than economic exchange, and may involve more real options and estimates of 'opportunity costs'. There is no agreement in advance about what is to be exchanged, defaulters are not subject to the same automatic sanctions. (On the other hand, claims are not transferable.) Social exchange is less certain and predictable, more ambiguous and subtle, than economic exchange. Members of communities may be surprised by the gifts they receive from fellow members and the returns they make may astonish the donors. The operation of social exchange depends on a notion of social balance or reciprocity, the moral obligation to repay favours even when they were unsolicited.[3] In some cultures the weight of this obligation is especially strong and the power of those who give gifts correspondingly great. The Japanese are notably wary of the bearer of gifts: they have a keen appreciation of the consequent indebtedness.[4] A kind man will have more delicacy than to give gifts to his friends. A considerate man inflicts gifts only on his enemies. Anthropologists have shown how the powerful man in many non-literate societies is the generous man: he has a superfluity of goods and services which he can bestow on others; historians have shown how the successful warrior, like William of Normandy, has consolidated his power not only by the demonstration of military might, but by the distribution of spoils.[5]

Exchange theory does not provide a complete explanation of power and authority in schools, although the paucity of goods and services available for exchange helps to account for their being underpowered. The basis of authority lies in conquest – in the form of Forster's Education Act of 1870, which took the first step towards compulsory education. Before this time a variety of inducements and bribes were necessary to keep children at school under the authority of the teacher. Sunday schools, ragged schools and the early elementary schools relied heavily on prizes, gifts given in return for submission to the rule of the school. The basic power structure of the school today resembles the paradigm of conquest rather than that of the free market.[6]

When gifts are in short supply, a variety of unlikely commodities may be pressed into service for purposes of exchange. Goffman has described how cigarettes and objects of little intrinsic worth are hoarded by hospital inmates for use in social exchange. 'Social exchanges in the hospital were characterized by the meager resources the patients had for expressing mutual regard and extending mutual aid.'[7] Gifts from outside were not consumed but used to cement social bonds. Blau has shown how, in a federal law enforcement agency, asking more competent colleagues for advice was used as a 'gift'.[8] In their relationships with their colleagues and headmaster, teachers probably find this gift too costly: the tradition of self-sufficiency makes any admission of deficiency in pedagogic skills expensive.

Power derives from social imbalance. A donor upsets social equilibrium unless he is repaying a debt or making a gift within various social categories which are defined as standing outside normal exchange relationships – the very young (though they may have to pay off the debt in later years), the very old (though they may be using up accumulated balances), or the very inferior, who do not enter the scales against the donor in any case. The headmaster who promotes to a departmental headship a man who has earned it, merely restores the social balance; but, if he can promote a man who has not earned it, he has tipped the balance decisively in his own favour: the promoted man can be expected to spend the rest of his career discharging his obligation. (Men of little merit have been given peerages, at least since the famous 'Tory Dozen' in the reign of Queen Anne, for similar purposes and with similar consequences.) The headmaster who is tempted into such an exchange must weigh against its advantages in power its possible disadvantages in incompetence.

There are few controlled and systematic studies of the connection between social exchange and power relations in English schools, although Cohen has investigated the behaviour of pupil teachers during their period of school practice in these terms. Cohen found that the educational beliefs and objectives of pupil teachers were closer to those of the class teacher with whom they had been placed than they were to those of the college tutor-supervisor. 'Low authoritarian' teachers in 'high authoritarian' schools learn to be more authoritarian in their approach to children. In this way, apparently, they placate the class teacher. Cohen describes the process as follows:

> In exchange for the support from the classteacher which allows her to perform adequately, the student has little to give in return except acts of gratitude and acknowledgement of the classteacher's skill in control. The more difficult the situation, the more frequent and less valued are the student's exchanges of gratitude with the classteacher. Undervalued exchanges no longer produce the desired support from the teacher and the student (against her wishes) must now exchange the more highly authoritarian behaviour valued by the classteacher.[9]

In short, tough teachers in tough schools need more than flattery from their apprentices: they want tough-minded effectiveness.

Teachers have little to give that anybody wants. They therefore pay a good deal of attention to 'motivating' their pupils – that is, to increasing their needs. Power exists when men have needs and the resources to meet these are scarce. Compliance is exchanged for gratification. The important needs that teachers meet are often extrinsic or long-range – pupils' needs for qualifications and good jobs on leaving school, parents' needs to have children taken off their hands. But pupils have important gifts to offer teachers: one of their most valuable gifts is not making a noise, especially when the headmaster, inspectors, or important visitors are around. Pupils' power is high under conditions of maximum visibility; their hold over teachers strong before an impending visitation. Their other important gift is to pass examinations and acquit themselves creditably in academic pursuits. The teacher whose pupils constantly make excessive noise and rarely pass examinations is in a precarious position. He is fully alive to this fact; so are his pupils.

Relationships among members of staff are also 'underpowered' because teachers have little of value to give to one another. The teacher with a good ration of free periods which he can surrender to colleagues who wish to have time off, is in a strong position; but, in general, interdependence is not a marked feature of school life. Teachers are able to function with little help from colleagues. The development of teamteaching is placing senior and more out-of-date teachers in a dependent relationship to their young and enterprising colleagues. As one report on team-teaching has put it:

> The younger teachers supplied freshness and originality of approach, the experienced teachers displayed great attention to the careful progression of their methods and the oldest members of the team realized how their conception of modern method had changed drastically for the better. On further reflection, the immediate benefit was probably greater for the staff than the pupils.[10]

But teachers are not dependent on team-teaching in the same way that scientists today are commonly dependent on a research team. They are able to function adequately without this organizational structure (though conceivably they may perform some tasks more adequately with it). Scientists must obtain the co-operation of their colleagues; but formal structures of hierarchical authority do not necessarily correspond with the gifts that scientists have to offer. A subordinate commonly has special and esoteric knowledge which is vital to his superiors; if he needs to protect his knowledge he can make it over-complicated and virtually incommunicable, thus maximizing his autonomy. It is recognized that formal seniority does not give actual power to enlist co-operation: 'Telling someone what to do is taboo. The greatest man in science cannot tell the lowest what to do.'[11] In these circumstances scientists make 'gifts' of information to their colleagues in return for recognition. (Professors may 'induce students or colleagues to assist them' by offering them the chance to publish joint papers.[12])

> Ordinarily the strains between individualism and interdependence are lessened by the exchange of gifts. The exchange not only permits both donor and recipient to retain their independence; it also ceremonially demonstrates their independence while simultaneously linking them in a solidary relationship.[13]

The dependence of scientists on one another puts power into the social system of science, often in an inverse direction to the formal hierarchy. A distinguished physicist, Professor L. Alvarez, has described how he re-established himself as an academic scientist at the age of forty, after a period as a senior scientific administrator:

> When I returned to Berkeley from Livermore I had no graduate students, and no apparent niche in the rapidly developing field of fundamental particle physics

He obtained two research students and made a deal with them:

> I would hire them as my research assistants for the next two years, as far as the personnel department was concerned, if they would treat me during that time, as if I were *their* research assistant. My biggest job was to convince them that I was serious, but after that, they assigned me homework problems, and let me help them with their experiments.[14]

When members of an organization can work relatively independently, co-operation is not an important gift, and non-co-operation is a feeble weapon. But in organizations with close-knit work groups, simply making mistakes may be a powerful technique whereby subordinates attack superiors. In schools only extreme inefficiency on the part of a teacher would seriously inconvenience his headmaster. In industry, having things go wrong interferes in an obvious and immediate way with production and profits;[15] in schools, the consequence of pedagogical mistakes may be long delayed or never come to light. Even if teachers were to 'go slow', most headmasters would probably never notice.

The conclusion of Turner's study of the organization of a secondary modern school was that, once the school was established and settled into a routine of work, the staff had little need of the headmaster and the headmaster still less of the staff. The head had no 'gifts' of particular worth to offer his assistants, and their gift of co-operation was one he could well do without:

> The schoolmaster has in fact few inducements to offer a headmaster; for although his co-operation is useful, his lack of it need not make much difference to a headmaster who has withdrawn from academic interests to administrative ones. Enough headmasters function happily enough in spite of non-co-operation by some staff.[16]

Teachers do not even need the headmaster as protector. The power of leaders has often rested on the protection they could give their followers. Bloch has interpreted the power structure of feudal Europe in these terms: as the kinship group proved inadequate to protect its members, feudal lords offered this service in return for submission. It is true that protection in itself was never a sufficient offering: material gifts were important too.

> The liberality of the chief towards his war-companions seemed so essential a part of the bond between them that frequently, in the Carolingian age, the bestowal of a few gifts – a horse, arms, jewels – was an almost invariable complement to the gesture of personal submission.... The only true master was he who had given presents to his dependants.'[17]

Bertrand de Jouvenal has similarly interpreted, and regretted, the great power of the modern state through its offer to protect. Modern nations are peopled in the main by 'securitarians' whose anxieties lead to an insistent demand for social security. 'Thus, all stands firm in the structure of the new State. There are no limits to the Minotaur's beneficent protection; there can be none, therefore, to his authority.[18]

It is true that teachers expect the headmaster to protect them against pupils, parents and the local education authority. The new headmaster, like the new manager of a gypsum plant described by Gouldner, must show that he can stand up to the head office. If the manager failed to stand his ground against head office pressures, 'workers viewed this pattern of behaviour as "unmanly". It created a situation in which they did not know where they stood, and in which they felt powerless.'[19] Teachers similarly expect their headmaster to show that he is a man *vis-à-vis* County Hall.

Protection against pupils and parents is perhaps more important in America than in England; it is given considerable emphasis by Becker in his study of Chicago teachers. He interpreted the internal organization of the school 'as a system of defenses against parental intrusion'. The school principal was expected to back up his teachers against pupils and parents 'regardless of circumstances'. The principal who failed to do so was regarded as a coward. He was expected daily to reaffirm his toughness, which was the bedrock of the classteacher's discipline. 'The teacher's authority, then, is subject to attack by pupils and may be strengthened or weakened depending on which way the principal throws the weight of his authority.'[20]

In 'Castle Secondary Modern School', England, this protective role of the head was important chiefly in the early days after the school was established. His most important gift to his staff was firm rule over the pupils, and thus an easier school to work in.

> His authority was accepted ... in appreciation of the positive benefits of his leadership in the early successes of the new school. He particularly obtained credit for the manner in which he solved initial discipline problems with pupils and made the job of teaching much easier for the staff.[21]

But compared with other types of organization, educational groups do not see 'protection' as a particularly important feature of their leader's job, even in America. Military, occupational, social and educational groups have been studied and compared with respect to the characteristics of their leaders. Subordinates in social groups give their leaders a high 'integration' score (they reduce conflict among members); subordinates in military groups give their leaders a low 'recognition' score (they do not often give approval to their followers); and subordinates in educational groups are notable for the low 'representation' score they give to their leaders (their leaders are not remarkable for representing them and defending them from attack).[22] In comparison with many other social and occupational groups teachers have less need of protection. Their minimal needs are no firm basis for headmasterly power.

Like the Stuart kings headmasters and their assistants derive much of their power not from enforcing rules, but from suspending them. Suspending and dispensing powers are not only the prerogative of kings, they are vital to the exercise of power in all organizations. When managers have no such discretion with regard to bureaucratic rules, their power is very seriously curtailed, as Crozier observed in a highly routinized French bureaucracy: 'They [the managers] cannot even permit a breach of the rules easily; thus they have no bargaining power in the most trivial matters.'[23] The gift that James II could offer Roman Catholics was the suspension of the Test Acts which kept them from public office; and neither the trial of the seven bishops who refused to distribute the Declaration of Indulgence nor the Bill of Rights of 1689 contested the right and need of rulers to make exceptions to rules. The Bill of Rights abolished suspending power (by which laws could be altogether placed in abeyance), but with regard to dispensing power – by which particular exceptions to laws can be made, as circumstances require – condemned it 'only as it hath been used and exercised of late'.[24] The issue of licences – to fish, drive cars, fly aeroplanes or shoot guns – is today the formal means of dispensing with general laws in favour of particular people.

In schools monitors, prefects, sixth-formers and members of the first fifteen may be licensed to disregard a variety of general rules relating to attendance at various school assemblies, use of particular rooms or areas of the school premises, wearing of articles of school uniform, entrance by particular doors, and the like. But licensing takes the rules out of the free market for bargaining purposes (unless they may be fairly easily revoked). School rules which a teacher may dispense with at any time for any individual, at his discretion, may be more effective tools of power. Both subordinates and superiors may use rules for protective purposes. Pupils often insist that the rules regarding homework be observed when a teacher with a heavy load of marking might prefer to waive them. Insistence on observing homework rules may be a more potent threat on the part of pupils than teachers. Schools which try to have few or no rules deprive pupils not only of powerful offensive weapons, but also of crucial defences: for in the absence of rules, excessive demands may be made upon them. And schools with few or no rules deprive teachers of valuable gifts which they can offer pupils. Thus the social bonding of the school is weakened and the interplay of teachers and taught is in danger of degenerating into a condition of stalemate.

In general, the rules that teachers are able to dispense with for particular individuals are not many and are fairly trivial. A teacher may allow a boy to miss games or morning assembly (once in a while), to leave (a little) early, or to do no prep. These exceptions are not wholly unimportant in the hour-by-hour, day-by-day relationships of school life. Like the industrial managers described by Gouldner, teachers can use rules for bargaining purposes to gain co-operation: 'In effect, then, formal bureaucratic rules served as a control device not merely because they provided a legitimating framework for the allocation of punishments, but also because they established a punishment which could be withheld.'[25] But the dispensing powers of teachers are not really very far reaching. If teachers were able to dispense with major rules, and to allow pupils to leave school at say twelve or thirteen instead of fifteen, or even to absent themselves for a month or so, their power would acquire a dimension of corresponding significance. And there is no reason why teachers, as expert advisers and assessors of their pupils, should not have the power to dispense with the law relating to the school leaving age. (And if they could, in appropriate cases, require their pupils to stay for some years after the age of fifteen, their power would be greater still.) The dispensing powers of teachers are at present too trivial to provoke the opposition of a single bishop or even seven parents.

It has been argued with respect to the American scene that society is not prepared to invest great power in teachers because the return on the investment is so uncertain. At best it is non-specific and long-term. Investing authority in a teacher is risky and, in consequence, he is given insufficient power to do his job. To be effective he needs to have some control over a wide range of circumstances, many external to the school, which are now known to have a crucial impact on educational effectiveness:

> Although he [the teacher] is responsible for demonstrating the progress of his students, he has little or no authority to control the environmental factors (social, political, and economic) that operate in and on the school and have a decided bearing on the progress of students and affect the realization of the teacher's goals. Moreover, he has little choice of curricula or textbooks, has nothing to do with assignment to ability groups, can do little more than suggest that a child may need psychiatric counselling and does not have the authority to curb severe behavioral problems by suspension or expulsion. For example, a teacher assigned a basic class consisting of emotionally disturbed

children, low-ability students, and discipline cases has no authority to control the innumerable variables that seriously affect the progress of these children, yet is responsible for each child's progress.[26]

In England the teacher may have more control over curricula and textbooks, but is otherwise an equally serious case of under-investment.

Pupils may be required to invest heavily in education; and in this circumstance lies the chance of the school to exert an influence over them. In return for the 'price' they are charged, pupils may accord their schools considerable power. The tendency in recent years has been substantially to lower the price.

When we look at those organizations which appear to have a profound influence (in the intended direction) on the behaviour of their members, we see that they are often demanding and exacting even in excess of what might seem necessary for the attainment of their goals. Pride in an organization and identification with its aims may arise from penalties as well as rewards. The soldier's pride in his regiment does not appear to be inversely related to the restrictions and even the humiliations to which he has been subjected; the professional pride of doctors and nurses has a similar relationship to the rigours and even the belittlement experienced during training. Long professional courses which contain obsolete and irrelevant syllabuses – much of the anatomy in a doctor's course, and the Roman law in a lawyer's – may constitute a price which is positively related to ascribed value. The contemporary cry for curricular 'relevance' is a cry for a still further reduction in the price of education.

Even those professional courses which have traditionally recruited many pre-socialized entrants are not notable for their lack of rigour and painful induction into professional codes. On the contrary, medical, legal, theological and military academies, which have tended to take the sons of men in these professional fields, are notable not for being lax, but exacting. They treat their students as if they were especially needful of socialization, when in fact a great deal of pre-socialization has probably occurred at home. Surplus rigour is the price they charge for membership.

In many societies, and in our own in the past, the price which the young were charged for entering society at all was high; and membership correspondingly valued. Apprenticeship was long, trying, and often futile.

The low value placed on joining adult society, and the disinclination to identify with it and support its values, appear to be prevalent in societies like affluent, middle-class California, where the price of entrance has been substantially lowered. The hippies have come from homes and schools in which parents and teachers have lost their nerve and have made few demands. The process of growing up has lost all semblance of the initiation ordeals by which communities have traditionally set a price on membership of the adult world.

Initiation procedures vary greatly in their nature and purpose in the societies that anthropologists have studied; and they have been variously interpreted, in psycho-analytical and in sociological terms. Sociologists have tended to de-emphasize the psychological aspects of initiation, the states of mind, perhaps the suffering, of the initiates. Initiation is seen as the dramatization of status transition, and is important for promoting and maintaining social solidarity. Its essential function is communication, the announcement of an individual's change of status in a public spectacular.[27]

More psychological interpretations of initiation rites have focused on the importance of detaching young males from their mothers and giving them a sense of masculine identity. Initiation is especially important not when social solidarity is in doubt, but when infants share their mother's bed to the exclusion of the father. Isolation from women and painful tests of manliness break any excessively strong dependence on the mother and ensure a young man's identification with adult males and acceptance of the male role. Above all, these ordeals emphasize the advantages of joining adult society.[28]

The twentieth-century progressive school is the antithesis of the initiation school – even in its European version, the Renaissance grammar school. The sixteenth-century grammar school was single-sex, it removed the boy from his family, it inflicted physical hardship, it offered life in a marginal environment, and it enforced a sharp break with the individual's past. By contrast, the progressive school today – and, indeed, schools in general, under the now pervasive influence of progressive ideas – stresses links with the family, the interpenetration of the school and its social context, the 'relevance' of its curriculum. It emphasizes sensitivity rather than toughness, co-operation rather than competition, domestic rather than military-monastic virtues. And its curriculum is de-Latinized. Latin was the core of the curriculum in the sixteenth century precisely because it emphasized discontinuity, irrelevance, a separate linguistic environment and the learning of secret meanings. The school had the characteristic of a Secret Society, and its special quality was its apartness. Flogging and the Stoic authors were a vital protection against effeminacy. The sixteenth-century grammar school had the main features of an initiation school, for

> Puberty rites are ... ceremonial inductions or initiations of the youth into extra-familial life which involve a sense of break with the past (a 'marginal environment') together with segregation from the family and from those of the other sex, and chastisement under the direction of elders for didactic purposes.[29]

The Renaissance boy at school was in little doubt that a high price was needed for his future place in society.

Coercion, says Etzioni, leads to alienation. American schools, on the evidence of surveys conducted in the nineteen-thirties, exercise predominantly normative controls, with coercion as a secondary source of compliance.

> Normative controls in schools include manipulation of prestige symbols, such as honours, grades, and citations; personal influence of the teacher; 'talks' with the principal; scolding and sarcasm, demanding 'apologies', and similar means which are based on appeals to the student's moral commitments and on manipulation of the class peer group's climate of opinion. Coercion has declined in significance over the last decades, for modern education de-emphasizes 'discipline' as a goal and stresses internalization of norms.[30]

'Levels of alienation are closely associated with the degree of coercion applied.'[31]

Etzioni's thesis is a serious over-simplification. Whether or not coercion alienates depends on the purposes of the school and the way in which pupils define the situation in which they find themselves. If they see their training as a preparation for difficult and arduous duties ahead, the 'manipulation of prestige symbols' as a form of control may be treated with derision. The headmaster's honours board or points system is a secret – perhaps even an open – joke.

The boys in the Palace School of the Grand Seraglio in the days of Suleiman the Magnificent had been abducted from their Christian homes. They had been separated from their families and were in school under duress. They were 'tribute boys', slaves who were expected not only to subscribe to the values of an alien society, but to fight to the death in their defence. (The field of Mohacs was only one of their more spectacular triumphs.) They showed little sign of 'alienation' – as Machiavelli[32] and other well-informed contemporaries testified. The morale of students was never higher. Their education in the Palace School was long, highly selective at successive stages, and exacting; it

> covered an average period of about twelve to fourteen years and combined in almost equal proportions instruction in the humanities of Islam, in physical training and the arts of war and government, and in manual training; it was one of the most formal, systematic, and arduous courses ever devised in preparation for a public career.[33]

With rigour went loyalty.

> So perfectly did the Palace School mould aliens of widely divergent race and creed to the Turkish type, and so thoroughgoing was the process of assimilation, that there are on record few instances of rebels or renegades among officials educated within its walls.[34]

The severities of a military academy preparing for the élite American Coast Guard corps have been described by Dornbusch. It is true that the drop-out rate was high (Dornbusch himself appears to have dropped out and remustered as a professor of sociology); but the clean break with the past, the 'loss of identity in terms of pre-existing statuses', and the hazing of 'swabs' appear to have been related to subsequent pride in the corps among those who survived. Early days in the academy were days of abasement, but 'The assignment of low status is useful in producing a correspondingly high evaluation of successfully completing the steps in an academic career....'[35]

Etzioni's hypothesis does not stand up well in the light of data from English boarding schools collected by Royston Lambert and his associates.

> We have found, in fact, that this [connection between coercion and alienation] does not always apply. Indeed, in one school where methods of control were those of the eighteenth century the application of a brine-stiffened lash to the backside produced high commitment among recipients, the marks being displayed later as a somewhat macabre proof of endurance to admiring peers.[36]

Pupils may object to authority 'going soft' and demand toughness, although, as Lambert points out, much will depend on whether they are in a training ship or a progressive boarding school. But pupils commonly demand rigour in learning and discipline. The function of the school is to provide a testing ground. Even the Spartan hippy communes of Oregon often have the appearance of self-imposed ordeals, young people putting themselves to the test because their schools have refused to do so.

There is experimental evidence on the 'price' paid for membership of an association and the value attached to it. Aronson and Mills conducted an experiment with female American university students in an attempt to answer the question: 'Is severity of initiation positively related to group preference when motivation for admission is held constant?' Women college students were randomly allocated to three discussion groups. For admission to one group, 'initiation' was severe in the form of reading embarrassing literature to the investigator as an alleged screening device; for admission to the second, initiation took the form of a much milder embarrassment test; for admission to the third there was no initiation at all. All participants in this (unwitting) experiment listened to the same boring and banal tape-recording supposedly of a discussion in the group they were going to join. Those who had endured a severe initiation rated this discussion much more favourably than those who had a mild initiation or none at all. These results were held to support the hypothesis that 'individuals who undergo an unpleasant initiation to become members of a group increase their liking for the group'.[37] In terms of Festinger's theory of 'cognitive dissonance',[38] people who have gone through a great deal of pain and trouble to attain something will be reluctant to concede that it was not really worth it, if that should prove to be the case: they will over-estimate its value to bring it into line with the effort they have expended. If what they have gained is membership of a not very attractive community, they will reduce their dissonance by exaggerating its appeal. Young women pursued in courtship have long known this simple rule.

Aronson and Mills argue that 'The initiation must be severe enough to constitute a genuine investment....' The argument, like the theory of social exchange, is couched in economic terms. (It has much in common with the older theological arguments by which victims of misfortune have found hidden blessings in their disasters, contrived by the will of God.) There is ample evidence in the autobiographies of the great that long anguish at a public school is by no means incompatible with great pride in that school in later life. Whether this is the case with ex-prisoners is less certain; although in criminal circles an especially arduous stretch on the Moor doubtless confers considerable prestige.

The value subsequently ascribed to an investment of great effort or endurance may depend in part on the status to which it eventually leads. Doctors, nurses, parsons and army officers may have suffered a protracted ordeal, but they have done quite nicely in the end. Goffman, discussing the lot of inmates in an asylum, talks of their 'proactive status' – the change in their social position which they can expect when they get out. He suggests that there will be pride in the institution that has inflicted mortification and abasement if the proactive status is generally held in high regard: 'When the proactive status is a relatively favourable one, as it is for those who graduate from officers' training schools, élite boarding schools, ranking monasteries, etc., then jubilant official reunions, announcing pride in one's "school", can be expected.'[39]

It is especially in these circumstances that schools, seminaries

Power, gifts and investment in education 45

and academies may exert a strong influence on their members after they have left. If they were put severely to the test whilst at school, but enjoy high status afterwards, the school's power over their adult behaviour may be considerable. They will find unsuspected virtue in the codes and values which were detestable at the time. They are changed by a process of retroactive socialization. Ex-servicemen who hated the army and were unremarkable for their military bearing are to be found erect on veterans' parades, and warning their colleagues in civilian life that 'you can't run an army like that'. Their later regimental pride would be a matter of profound astonishment to their former commanding officers.

4 Humour, sex and power

Humour and sex may be equally dangerous to authority. Either may deflect the most determined wielder of power from his course. Ruthlessly dedicated organizations like armies and monasteries have tended to be single-sex and solemn. The experienced schoolteacher recognizes the potential threat of humour and sex and suppresses manifestations of both. He knows that either leads quickly to the taking of liberties. Sex and humour may take the power out of schools as social and educational systems; but both may promote an extension of communication to difficult or risky topics and across age and status barriers. Jesters can make suggestions about dangerous and normally forbidden issues to their superiors; girls can often do likewise (when the superior is male). The result is greater flexibility and adaptability in social life. Both sex and humour may be especially valuable in this way in societies when the sense of honour is strong and sensitivity to personal slights acute. A proud society – whether a nation or a school – which is concerned to avoid dishonour, may be deeply offended by the mildest criticism; the offence is less when the critic is either a jester or a pretty girl. Schools which contain boys and girls and jesters may be adaptable and flexible; they are likely to lose their thrust and power.

In his book on *The Art of Teaching*, Gilbert Highet attaches great importance to humour among the characteristics of the good teacher. 'One of the most important qualities of a good teacher is humour. Many are the purposes it serves.'[1] Humour, says Highet, brings a teacher and his class closer together; and it is a bridge between the young and their seniors. If a subject does not naturally lend itself to humorous sallies, then humour must be contrived. 'Of course some subjects, notably the sciences, do not admit humorous treatment. There the wise teacher will continue to introduce flashes of humour extraneously....'[2] This advice is sound for the teacher of university and adult students; for the teacher of secondary school children it could be disastrous.

The maintenance of order and seemly conduct in class is for many teachers – and not only beginners – a precarious business.[3] They may use one form of humour, sarcasm, as a form of control; but good-natured humour which arises from the subject of a lesson, and is not directed against any member of the class, may have equally unfortunate consequences. Humour breaches control, and a teacher may have difficulty in plugging the tidal wave of laughter and merriment which greets his joke. Laughter is a permitted response to a joke; protracted laughter hides under the guise of legitimacy to disrupt a lesson. A joke legitimizes turbulence which a teacher may find it difficult to suppress. Humour is a commodity which the wise teacher of secondary school children uses sparingly.

Humour, like drink, is an important means of sanctioning deviant behaviour: outrageous conduct may be excused 'because he was drunk' or 'because he only did it in jest'. For this reason the clown or fool may be a person of power; and in a tyrannical society he may have great significance as the only important form of countervailing power. A despotic headmaster needs the corrective of a staffroom buffoon. It is through him that, at staff meetings, his more serious colleagues may make their most daring counter-suggestions.

Both schoolchildren and schoolteachers may find the jester in their midst a useful check on the power of their superiors. These are simply particular applications of the general principle that the institutionalized fool becomes a major error-correcting mechanism in a despotic order. The court fool of Renaissance Europe was often a very powerful man, with an important voice in the great political and matrimonial-diplomatic issues of the day. Enid Welsford has examined his significance: 'many of the fools at the German court were clever observant men, deeply engaged in the religious controversies of the time'.[4] Often they were scheming and malicious, although Shakespeare's fools, especially Feste and Touchstone, were more benevolent and benign. Both claimed and exercised the jester's privilege of licensed criticism. Lear's fool likewise saw and spoke the truth about the men of power around him; but Feste exercised a more active power, planning the downfall of the arch-bureaucrat, Malvolio.

The court jester disappeared with the Stuarts and belief in the Divine Right of kings; he survived where authoritarian regimes lasted longer, for instance, in Tsarist Russia. When potentates exercise unbridled power, the fool is one of the few permitted sources of criticism and checks on folly. School councils will make a late-twentieth-century Stalky superfluous.

For schoolboys and schoolteachers, as for many others in subordinate positions, clowning is only a latent role; but they may treat even their dominant or manifest role humorously, and this, too, is a source of power. 'Effortless superiority' has been claimed by many when their superiority was based in fact on long and diligent study. Schoolboys may take their schooling lightly, even flippantly; their achievement only shows their easy mastery of their role obligations. Goffman has called such apparent indifference to role demands 'role-distance'[5] – standing apart from one's role yet performing it consummately. Solemn hard work and application to one's job is simply an indication that it requires all one's efforts. Flippancy is an aspect of the public school tradition (among both pupils and staff) which has received little attention. It is probably an important mechanism for maintaining and demonstrating one's independence of onerous and severely circumscribing role obligations. Role distance behaviour has been shown, in the case of jazz musicians, to have precisely this function: it is 'an adaptive strategy, whereby the performer can more or less fulfil his role obligations while maintaining his self-respect.'[6] In humorous or casual treatment of our roles we assert that we are not defined by them, that we are autonomous. We assert our independence and power.[7] The amateurishness of the English scholarly tradition is perhaps explicable as a defence against scholastic autocracy.

The ritual clown of the Hopi Indians is allowed to violate nearly every social taboo, including incest.[8] Even unofficial clowns, in classrooms and staffrooms, will be allowed to exceed the normal bounds of propriety, to engage in experimental behaviour, testing out new forms of conduct which challenge established practice. The joker can take liberties, ask for unthought-of privileges, suggest that sacred rules be abandoned, call into question hallowed procedures. The jester is 'putting out feelers', asking for information on taboo subjects; his apparently frivolous suggestion may be taken seriously. 'Joking provides a useful channel for covert communication on taboo topics' – such as death, staff incompetence and indignities to patients in hospitals.[9] In schools, jester-pupils may even comment adversely to their teachers about other teachers; they may suggest that they be let off homework or cross-country running; they may elicit advance information about promotions and demotions, punishments and examination marks. The listener has the job of transposing the joke to a serious level, of accepting its latent purpose. The headmaster in a staff meeting might accede to the jocular suggestion that Speech Days be abolished. The jester is often negotiating a private agreement to suspend usually operative rules.

Humour, like flirtation, makes proposals possible without loss of face or dignity if the proposal is rejected. 'The significance of the transaction in which humour is first acknowledged lies in the possibility of commenting on a taboo topic without a catastrophic degree of social disruption.'[10]

The humorous proposer who has been rejected can always say he didn't really mean it. A humourless society, especially if it is also a dignified society, must find other, perhaps more formal, means of making risky proposals. In schools which lack dignity and a strong sense of hierarchy, non-humorous suggestions are possible. 'Cheek' need not be camouflaged as jest. 'Rudeness', as Hargreaves found at Lumley Secondary Modern School, is a normal mode of communication.[11]

The traditional Japanese culture as described by Ruth Benedict illustrates the obstacles to communication in a society which is not only humourless but honourable. 'It is hard for us to realize the deadly seriousness that attaches to light remarks in Japan.'[12] The go-between is a substitute for humour in delicate transactions in which one runs the risk of rebuff. 'An intermediary is required in any situation where a man might feel shame if he fell short and consequently go-betweens serve on a great number of occasions – negotiating marriage, offering one's services for hire, leaving a job and arranging countless everyday matters.'[13]

The jester may in some circumstances become a scapegoat: he is then used to reaffirm prevailing values rather than to challenge them.[14] A class may round on a disruptive jester as a means of supporting the teacher; a staff meeting may turn on a flippant colleague to show their solidarity with the head.[15] But more commonly the clown will serve a contrary purpose, challenging lightly, tentatively and circuitously where bluntness and directness would provoke unyielding opposition. The community most open to new and unusual ideas is likely to be both humorous and dishonourable. Its problem may be to sustain any course of action before a fresh jocular or outrageous proposal deflects it onto yet another new course. Experimental evidence supports the commonsense observation that exposure to humour decreases feelings of anxiety and anger.[16] Defensiveness is diminished. So, too, is resolution. The determined and resolute pursuit of goals like open scholarships is probably best achieved in undeviating solemnity.

The co-educational school may also find itself deflected from serious academic purposes. The mixed school is academically underpowered. This is not because boys and girls pay more attention to each other than they do to their lessons; indeed, the label 'mixed' is probably something of a misnomer. The reason probably lies in the interpersonal relationships of men teachers and girl pupils. The mixed school is generally more relaxed, humane and tolerant than the single-sex school; and precisely for that reason may be less academically effective. It is apparently more relaxed and humane for girls than it is for boys; and it is the attainments of girls that appear to suffer. The choice, as so often in education, is between humanity and success.[17]

There seems to be little doubt that in general both pupils and teachers enjoy co-educational more than single-sex schools. This is the conclusion from inquiries among pupils and teachers who have had experience of both. Dale questioned college of education students who had attended both types of school; they recalled with greater satisfaction the nature of the discipline and of staff–pupil relationships generally in their co-educational schools.[18]

Humour, sex and power 51

When criticism was levelled at the discipline of co-educational schools it was on the ground that it was too lax; criticism of discipline in single-sex schools was on the ground of its severity.

> Clearly there was much more physical punishment of boys in the boys' schools than of boys in the mixed schools, nor do we find in the mixed schools the silence bells which seem to regulate the day in some girls' schools. There was also in many girls' schools – but not in all – a multiplicity of rules, often termed 'trivial' and 'petty' and 'unnecessary', rarely mentioned in the mixed schools.[19]

But girls appeared to gain the greater advantage in this respect from co-education:

> the women ex-pupils consistently record a greater satisfaction with the co-educational school (regarding discipline) than with the girls' schools, the male ex-pupils giving a similar opinion with a narrower gap between boys' and mixed schools which occasionally becomes equality.[20]

In fact, boys seemed to gain little if anything. Ex-pupils were asked to recall the friendliness of their teachers; females recalled greater friendliness in mixed schools, but males did not recall significantly more friendliness.[21] They were also asked to recall the helpfulness of teachers, and again females remembered teachers in their mixed schools as more helpful, but for males there was no significant difference.[22] Females recalled more 'over-fussiness' in their single-sex schools, but no such great disparity between the two types of school was recollected by the males.[23]

All the indications are that girls in secondary schools moderate the power or drive of their male teachers; boys in secondary schools have no such effect on their male or female teachers. Inquiries among pupils in mixed schools showed that girls in particular appreciated being taught by the opposite sex.[24] Eighty-six per cent of female juniors and 90 per cent of female seniors endorsed the 'good influence' of masters; but only 51 per cent of male juniors and 55 per cent of male seniors endorsed the 'good influence' of female teachers. It is a mistake to regard a co-educational school as the same environment for its male and female pupils. The relationship between 17-year-old boys and women teachers of forty is likely to be profoundly different from the relationship of 17-year-old girls and men teachers of forty.

It seems probable that the demands made on girls in co-educational schools may not be as demanding as in single-sex schools, both in the field of general deportment and academic attainment. In the co-educational schools girls complained comparatively infrequently about rules concerning school uniform, carrying satchels and wearing berets. 'Is it because [the schools] can ensure a satisfactory standard of dress and of good manners without recourse to such detailed rules, or are they satisfied with a less high standard in these matters?'[25] Research provides no answer to this question.

And it may be of little consequence that school hats are discarded for berets; of greater consequence would be a falling off in scholastic performance. Inquiries on this point are complicated and rightly hedged about with qualifications and warnings of methodological pitfalls. But when all allowance has been made for the difficulties of comparing mixed and single-sex schools with regard to academic attainments, the indications are that boys in mixed schools may do no worse and will often do better; girls will commonly do worse.

A number of studies carried out since the nineteen-twenties point to this conclusion. Tyson analysed the results of the J.M.B.'s School Certificate examinations held in 1925 and 1926 and concluded that: 'In general the boys from co-educational schools obtain better examination results than the boys from boys' schools: but the girls from co-educational schools do not fare quite so well as the girls educated in girls' schools.'[26] In the mid-thirties Field conducted an inquiry on a smaller scale in the Birmingham area and concluded that co-educated girls had a generally lower level of attainment in the School Certificate examinations than girls in single-sex schools; in the case of boys there was very little difference.[27] Both these investigations are fully alive to possible explanations in terms of the age of examinees and the selection of pupils with different social and personal characteristics to mixed and single-sex schools.

A more compelling and technically sophisticated study was made by Sutherland in Northern Ireland using the results of the Senior Certificate Examination of 1957.[28] The performance of candidates in ten subjects was examined; co-educated boys tended to have higher average scores than boys educated in single-sex schools, but the opposite was the case with girls. (When schools were taken as the units of comparison, substantially similar results were obtained.)

Co-educational schools often enter their pupils for examinations at a slightly earlier age than girls' schools; and they tend to draw a higher proportion of their pupils from poorer social backgrounds. Both these circumstances may unduly depress their examination results. Sutherland examined her data in the light of the age and social background of her subjects; neither factor appeared to have influenced the results. Moreover, as Sutherland observes, co-educated boys also come from poorer homes more often than boys in single-sex schools. 'If lower attainment were to be expected from those with fathers in the lower occupational groups, this factor should lower the results of the co-ed boys as well as of the co-ed girls'.

In three papers published since 1962 Dale has carefully and critically reviewed research conducted in this area. He has pointed to the effects of possibly inferior teachers in co-educational schools and of the tendency of co-educational schools to enter their pupils for more subjects and at a slightly earlier age. In his two earlier papers[29] he referred to the tendency in girls' schools for weaker subjects to be dropped and hence for examination results to be, in a sense, 'spuriously' good. Dale has an avowed sympathy with co-educational schools and naturally wants to see the best in them.

He has properly given Sutherland's work very close and critical attention; he has re-worked many of her data; he has even repeated her inquiry in Northern Ireland in 1959, with special reference to attainment in English (both Literature and Language). His results are substantially the same as Sutherland's. But whereas in his earlier papers he had argued that girls in single-sex schools might appear to do well because they drop their weaker subjects, he now infers that girls in mixed schools appear to do badly in English because they drop a strong one, namely English Literature. This ingenious argument is based on the good results (in co-educational schools) of girls taking English Language who did not take the Literature paper. The argument rests on an assumed correlation between ability in literature and language which Dale concedes is 'far from perfect'. If girls in single-sex schools drop their weaker subjects, the reason is not hard to see; why girls in co-educational schools should drop their stronger subjects is impossible to see.[30]

The generally poorer performance of girls in co-educational schools compared with girls in single-sex schools is probably not explained by the distracting presence of boys. There is some evidence that in mixed boarding schools boys find girls a distraction;[31] but if this is so in day-schools, it does not seem to impair their academic performance. The interaction of boys and girls in the same school is probably an irrelevance; indeed, interaction seems to a surprising extent not to happen. The evidence of sociometric studies points to a remarkable cleavage, virtually two societies in parallel.

> Sex. This is undoubtedly the most important divisive factor in children's school groups, at least between the ages of nine and fifteen. Every investigator of mixed classes ... has emphasized its paramount importance, so much so that one wonders whether the adjective 'mixed' is not rather misleading.[32]

The relationships which would repay further investigation are those between male teachers and their female pupils on the one hand and their male pupils on the other. Social researchers are well aware that when they wish to reduce the power and resistance of a male interviewee they are wise to send along an interviewer who is young and female. The differential treatment of girls and boys in mixed schools by members of staff would be a delicate but fruitful area of research. Opposite-sex attractiveness, like humour, may at least temporarily deflect a master from his resolve to see that difficult work is done.

5 Power and the shape and size of schools

When we look at schools today two tendencies are evident: they are getting bigger in size and more open in design. Both tendencies increase the power of people in superordinate positions. The boss who has many subordinates is likely to be more powerful than the boss who has few; the boss who can see his subordinates is more powerful than the boss who cannot. The assistant teacher is likely to lose power on both counts; and moreover, while schools grow in size, the class diminishes. The class teacher's 'subordinates' are fewer in number. It is by no means necessarily the case that large classes (of thirty or forty pupils) are more difficult to control than classes of nine or ten: a large class has more difficulty in achieving the unity required for effective opposition. Large schools, small classes and open-plan architecture may increase the power of headmasters and reduce that of their assistants.

Superiors who can keep their subordinates under observation and communicate easily and rapidly with them are in a position of great strength. Modern organizational theorists have pointed to the importance of 'visibility' for authority relationships and the severity of punishment. When a person in charge of a group is visible to his superiors, he will usually be more restrictive and autocratic, he will show that he is effectively in command, and he will tend to punish infractions of his rule more rigorously: 'The more visible the violation, the more severe and persistent the sanctions.'[1] This discovery of modern organizational analysts was evident more than a century ago to Jeremy Bentham. He feared that the open-plan school which he proposed would so increase visibility that pupils would be massively constrained and stripped of any vestige of autonomy.

Bentham's 'panopticon' was an educational broiler-house. It was to be a circular building with open cells on the circumference and an inspection point at the centre. It would be the most effective design for prisons, hospitals, factories and schools: 'Morals reformed – health preserved – industry invigorated – instruction diffused – public burthens lightened – Economy seated, as it were, upon a rock – the Gordian knot of the Poor-Laws not cut, but untied – all by a simple idea in Architecture.'[2]

Bentham feared only that his plan would be too efficacious, that it might quite rightly be attacked for 'its tendency to introduce tyranny into the abodes of innocence and youth'. The dominance of the teacher would be assured: 'All play, all chattering – in short, all distraction of every kind, is effectually banished by the central and covered situation of the master, seconded by partitions or screens between the scholars, as slight as you please.' On the other hand, these arrangements would make it possible to cater for individual differences:

> The different measures and casts of talent, by this means rendered, perhaps for the first time, distinctly discernible, will indicate the different degrees of attention and modes of culture most suitable to each particular disposition; and incurable and irreproachable dullness or imbecility will no longer be punished for the sins of idleness and obstinacy.

Bentham thought that the sheer effectiveness of his proposals might lead some to ask 'whether the liberal spirit and inquiry of a free citizen would not be exchanged for the mechanical discipline of a soldier, or the austerity of a monk? – and whether the result of this high-wrought contrivance might not be constructuring a set of machines under the similitude of men?'

Winchester has, in fact, precisely such a high-wrought contrivance which has, apparently, considerable potency. Winchester hall has been described as follows:

> The boys' flat-topped desks are fixtures standing sideways to the wall, with a cupboard and bookshelves up against the wall

and a six-foot partition between one desk and the next. As he sits at the desk the Wykehamist can look to the side and see what is going on within the hall, but he learns to withdraw into his recess....

College, the boarding house for the seventy scholars, has the same type of organization.... The impact of this intellectual powerhouse can scarcely be exaggerated.[3]

Until the middle of the nineteenth century the typical school was 'open-plan' in the sense that all the pupils and their teachers worked in a single, unpartitioned room or hall. 'Here each master sat with the boys of his form on benches curving round him, the senior master nearest the fire. There were groups in each corner, with others filling the gaps as necessary at strategic points along the sides.'[4] The single, all-purpose schoolroom was to be found when numbers were as high as three hundred, as at mid-century Marlborough: 'there was for many years only one room for the three hundred boys to spend their working hours in; and this room, in which they had to work during lesson times and play during their leisure, was warmed by a couple of open fires ... the smaller boys would never see the fire except from their remote desks.'[5] Status of both boys and staff was measured by distance from the fire rather than by the privacy and sumptuousness of separate rooms.

Specialization and the division of labour in teaching called for separate rooms. In the later nineteenth century they were often makeshift – the 'Dog Kennel' at Eton and the 'Turret Room' at Harrow: garrets, attics and outbuildings were called into use to meet the needs of particular subjects. Separate and private accommodation both expressed and reinforced the growing power and boundedness of the diverse subjects in the curriculum. Separate, private and even remote accommodation has often been provided to meet the needs of a rapidly expanding school population: and annexes for woodwork, domestic science, history or remedial teaching have sometimes appeared to flourish as deviant subcultures, separate centres of power, housing cliques of teachers making their own tea during the morning break, seldom seen in the main common room. The exigencies of the school building programme after World War II accelerated a movement towards pluralism of power which had begun for academic reasons. Remote and invisible, teachers in annexes and prefabricated huts have probably made distinctive and idiosyncratic contributions to educational practice.

Architects today are reinterpreting educational theory and practice and providing school buildings to give their interpretation expression. In 1956 the Ministry's Development Group made a detailed study of junior school requirements. 'In this and previous investigations, the architects had observed a new relationship between teachers and children and a blurring of divisions between one subject and another, between theoretical and practical work and between one lesson period and the next.' In consequence, these remarkably perceptive architects conceived the 'teaching area' as 'the whole school environment, rather than a series of individual rooms'.[6] Various open-plan schools have been built to reflect and encourage the removal of boundaries between tasks, subjects, teachers and pupils. (The notion of a boundary is one of the most frowned on in contemporary educational thought.) At Amersham, Finmere, the Eveline Lowe Primary School, Southwark, Vittoria School, Islington, and others, new school architecture expressly promotes 'flexibility' and accessibility.

Bernstein sees these boundary-removing operations as symptoms of a new principle of social integration, of a shift from mechanical to organic solidarity. However that may be, he is clear about its implications for the authority of teachers. 'Schools' boundary relations, both within and without, are now more open. This can be seen at many levels. First of all, the very architecture of the new schools points up their openness compared with the old schools. The inside of the institution has become more visible.' The significance of these architectural innovations for the status of teachers is clear: 'We are moving from secondary schools where the teaching roles were insulated from each other, where the teacher had an assigned area of authority and autonomy, to secondary schools where the teaching role is less autonomous and where it is a shared or co-operative role.'[7] The considerable degree of autonomy that teachers have enjoyed in the privacy of their separate classrooms is undermined by educational architects; and the danger is that our schools will be characterized by timidity, uniformity and mediocrity. The open school is likely to house a stale and routinized progressivism.

Schools have not only been changing their shape since the later nineteenth century: they have also increased in size. But they are more stable in numbers, and their growth can be managed and predicted. Because schools are larger, less transitory and more stable, the power of the headmaster tends to increase, although the power he enjoys will depend in some measure on the stage of growth of his particular school and of the whole school system. The greater power of the head in a large school, perhaps especially his greater freedom of manœuvre in deploying his more numerous subordinates, may help to account for the greater effectiveness of large schools in attaining their formal academic goals.

In mid-Victorian England grammar schools were large with a hundred pupils. (The major public schools tended to be bigger: Eton had over 800 pupils when the Clarendon Commission reported on the public schools in 1864; Winchester had 200.) Typical of the endowed grammar schools were Nottingham High School, reported by the Taunton Commission in 1868 to have 95 pupils, Queen Mary's Grammar School, Walsall 119, and Felsted School 95. The average size of grammar schools had apparently risen steeply between 1820 and the eighteen-sixties: 35 schools for which there is exact information for the earlier date in the *Digest of Schools and Charities* had an average of 40 pupils; half a century later their average size was 108.[8]

With the rapid growth of wealth, population, easier travel and cities in late-Victorian England, schools grew in size. The seven major public schools investigated by the Clarendon Commission in 1864 had on average 328 pupils; in 1895, when the Bryce Commission reported, they had 514. (The average size of the 400 Preparatory Schools which existed in 1900 was only 34.) Proprietary schools grew little between the eighteen-sixties and the 'nineties, from an average size of 185 to 193; but the new higher-grade elementary schools in the large cities contained on average, no fewer than 592 pupils in 1895.[9] But a significant number of maintained secondary schools with more than five or six hundred pupils did not appear until the mid-twentieth century. By the early nineteen-sixties 2,285 out of 5,847 maintained secondary schools had fewer than 400 pupils, but 297 had between 800 and 1,000 and 127 had more than a thousand.[10]

Mid-Victorian schools were not only smaller, they were far less stable than today. Their numbers could fluctuate dramatically over a relatively short period of time, especially when they experienced a change of headmaster. While Bedford School rose in numbers from 41 pupils in 1820 to 194 in 1868, Sherborne from 19 to 187, Wolverhampton Grammar School from 60 to 157, the Taunton Commission found 50 ancient endowed grammar schools 'in abeyance'. Numbers at Westminster and Shrewsbury were falling at the time of the Clarendon Commission's inquiries. Private and proprietary schools, which multiplied rapidly after 1820, had even less stability. While some rose steadily in numbers, others fluctuated and finally closed their doors. Out of more than a hundred proprietary schools founded in the first half of the nineteenth century, at least a dozen had ceased to exist by the eighteen-sixties.[11]

Headmasters will generally be less powerful during a period of rapid expansion: their assistants can easily find jobs elsewhere. When the school population expanded rapidly in the nineteen-fifties, and college and university populations likewise in the nineteen-sixties, heads of institutions were obliged to moderate any tendency they might have towards autocratic rule: their success was even measured by the proportion of their staff that they could keep. As expansion levels off and consolidation takes place, headmasters need not so sedulously woo their assistants. Powerful and autocratic headmasters appear to have flourished in periods of relative stability, at the end of Victoria's reign and in the inter-war years.

Fluctuating numbers, like rapidly rising numbers, also tend to promote democratic leadership. It is true that when the size of a school rapidly fluctuates, assistant staff are insecure; but these circumstances also call for organizational flexibility and adaptability. Fixed rules and regulations and a hierarchical chain of command depend on the expectation of recurrent and regular activities. Authoritarian rule is made easier under conditions of stability and established routine.[12]

Children (and staff) may feel lost, neglected and overwhelmed in very large schools. But the inquiries that have been carried out into the effects of an organization's size on its members have not shown a straightforward relationship between size and members' sense of belonging and strength of attachment. 'Alienation', when it occurs, seems to arise from some of the consequences of size – notably 'bureaucratization' – rather than from any intimidating characteristic of size itself.

Bureaucracy has many faces; they are not all inevitable accompaniments of size. A disproportionate increase in the proportion of administrative staff is commonly taken as an indicator of bureaucratization. Various investigations have shown that it is only in an organization's early stages of growth that increase in size is associated with large increases in the proportion of administrative personnel. Writing of industrial organizations Blau and Scott maintained that 'bureaucratization as indicated by the proportion of administrative personnel is, contrary to prevailing impressions, not directly related to size, and may even be inversely related to it.'[13]

What is remarkable about the contemporary school is that it has grown and remained pre-bureaucratic according to this particular indicator. A large secondary school will commonly have only a secretary, clerical grade, as a full-time bureaucrat. At the beginning of the twentieth century, administrative employees numbered less than 10 per cent of the production workers in British industry; half a century later they were 20 per cent.[14] The education service as a whole probably experienced a similar growth in administrative staff compared with production workers (teachers); but the growth was located outside the schools, in the offices of the local authorities. Direct-grant and independent schools have not even experienced, on any significant scale, such displaced or hidden bureaucratization. A large independent school will still manage its affairs with a bursar and assistant bursar as the only full-time professional administrators. The former colleges of advanced technology, by contrast, bureaucratized themselves rapidly after elevation to university status: the departments of the registrar, bursar and accountant have been major growth points. It may be that internal democracy, with its elaborate committee requirements and information systems, is a major cause of bureaucratization in educational institutions. As indicated by the proportion of full-time administrative personnel on the premises, the contemporary school is remarkably under-bureaucratized. But with the end of autocratic rule there will be committees with minutes, agenda and supporting documents: organizational democracy depends on keeping and communicating records of joint decisions and transactions. Bureaucracy can be confidently expected to rise in the schools on the grave of autocracy.

The proportion of administrative personnel in an organization is only a crude measure of the extent to which it has become bureaucratized. Two other features of bureaucracy may be more closely associated with organizational size: the hierarchical structure of authority and the application of impersonal rules. An American study of school size and bureaucratization in this more embracing Weberian sense shows a modest but significant association (correlation 0·43).[15] While there was a general tendency for large schools to be especially bureaucratic, this was not invariably the case (otherwise, of course, the correlation would have been unity). Out of twenty schools investigated one of the largest was the least, and two of the smallest were the most, bureaucratic. Size may be particularly irksome to members when its consequence is an inflexible application of universalistic, affectively neutral rules.[16]

A number of studies of behaviour in small groups have indicated that leaders become more authoritarian as the group becomes bigger. Leadership styles in large groups (more than thirty members) are task-centred, less concerned with affective relationships.[17] Cohen's investigations of the behaviour of headmasters in 343 English schools show that headmasters in large schools have a more bureaucratic (and in many ways a more 'authoritarian') conception of their role than headmasters in small schools.

Headmasters today are generally concerned to emphasize that they are not autocrats, that they wish to communicate and consult with their assistants and with parents.[18] Nevertheless, headmasters of large schools (more than three hundred pupils) tend to place greater stress on the legal authority of the headteacher. Irrespective of whether their schools are infant, junior or secondary, they give more support than the heads of small schools to the view that staff should 'carry out the headteacher's decisions even when they believe them to be unsound'. They also give greater emphasis to the application of rules and regulations to govern procedures: they give stronger support to the view that headteachers should 'insist that children's personal record cards be kept up-to-date by teachers and secretarial staff', and that they should 'require records or forecasts of every teacher's work'. Large-school heads do not place greater stress on the maintenance of hierarchically ordered authority systems in their schools; but the general picture is that the size of the school is significantly related to bureaucratized role conceptions on the part of the headteacher.[19]

Large schools are not necessarily more complex than small schools, but they will tend to be. They can offer a more elaborate curriculum, which calls for regulation and co-ordination. There is another feature of large schools which may make the formulation of explicit rules more important: the large school is likely to be more heterogeneous in its membership. Again, this is not necessarily the case. Large schools have often, by accident or design, recruited members (both pupils and staff) who share one or more important social characteristic. They may come from the same church, neighbourhood, social level, or ethnic group. In these circumstances there are many shared understandings, common values and assumptions about what is proper and acceptable behaviour: there is no need to spell out in detail what everybody takes for granted. But in a school, or any other community, which is not culturally homogeneous, there is a greater need to spell out rules and procedures.[20] Explicit codes of conduct become important. When social clubs, professions or schools open their doors more widely their regulations will usually become more numerous and precisely stated. Democracy in this sense, too, leads to bureaucracy.

It may be the more heterogeneous character of the large school, as well as the problem of coping with large numbers, which makes it a more autocratic organization. In large schools teachers need to be restrained by explicit regulations from the exercise of autocratic power. This is the conclusion of a careful and expert inquiry published by the National Foundation for Educational Research in 1952. An 'index of restriction' was constructed, based on the references in the regulations of local education authorities to restrictions on a teacher's liberty to inflict corporal punishment. Teachers in large county boroughs and densely populated urban areas apparently needed to be restrained far more than teachers in small county boroughs and rural areas. Only 9 per cent of the counties had a high index of restriction, compared with 30.8 per cent of county boroughs; and among the county boroughs, 65 per cent of those with a population in excess of 150,000 had a high index, but only 20 per cent of those with a smaller population.[21]

But the distinguishing feature of would-be punitive schools was not their urban situation but their size. The larger schools, whether in urban or rural areas, reported higher proportions of 'difficult children'. The larger schools tended to be in densely populated urban areas; but irrespective of area, the data indicated a significant correlation between the index of restriction and average size of school.[22] In large schools teachers suffer more provocation from 'difficult children' – who have many of the characteristics of the 'alienated workers' who appear in the literature on organizational size, bureaucracy and workers' attachment.[23]

Members of organizations, whether workmen in factories or pupils in schools, are not necessarily 'alienated' and made difficult and troublesome by the organization's size and its consequent bureaucratization and impersonality: much depends on what they are hoping to get from their membership. If they are seeking primarily warm, friendly and informal relationships they may not find a large organization to their taste; but if they are mainly concerned to achieve instrumental goals (high wages in factories, examination success in schools), impersonal and finely co-ordinated activity effectively directed to these ends may enhance their motivation and morale.

Goldthorpe found little evidence of 'alienation' among the workmen in the assembly departments of the Luton plant of Vauxhall Motors Ltd, yet they were employed in a large-scale enterprise characterized by impersonal relationships. Labour turnover and absenteeism were at a relatively low level. The men did not belong to cohesive work-groups, but they did not feel deprived on this score: they had not taken up their employment for matiness, but for cash; the satisfactions they sought at work were essentially 'instrumental' rather than 'expressive'. Nor were they bothered by the remoteness and impersonality of their supervisors, for 'the man who sees his work primarily as a means to extrinsic ends will have far less need for approval and commendation so far as the workplace is concerned, and will thus be able to accept with some equanimity supervisory behaviour of a remote and impersonal kind'.[24]

As with factories, so with schools: some pupils are seeking mainly instrumental, others mainly expressive satisfactions, and the former may find large, impersonal rule-regulated schools congenial. There are clear indications in the author's research that grammar school pupils are seeking much more instrumental satisfactions than are secondary modern school pupils. In his attempt to estimate the type and extent of the demand that pupils make on their schools, he concluded that the demand of modern school pupils is 43 per cent instrumental, 57 per cent expressive; by contrast the demand of grammar school pupils is 55 per cent instrumental and only 45 per cent expressive. The grammar school pupils found their schools less instrumental than they would have wished, the modern school pupils found their schools more.[25] Highly academic pupils and students, primarily interested in the acquisition of knowledge and examination success, may not find large, impersonal schools, colleges and universities distasteful. On the contrary, such organizations may most satisfactorily meet their needs.

This may help to account for the superior academic achievement of large schools. Their superiority is well supported in analyses of O-level, and especially A-level and open scholarship examination results, and may result from their impersonal, bureaucratic organization which able and instrumental pupils find congenial; from the more varied and flexible curricular provision which a large school can make; and from the more effective use of power that is possible to the headmaster of a large establishment.

Pedley suggested that school size, especially the size of the sixth form, was related to educational efficiency. An efficient sixth form should offer twenty subjects; and with eight to twelve pupils in every class of a two- or even three-year sixth form course, the minimum size of a sixth form would be 120 pupils.[26] Pedley produced no hard evidence that the size of a sixth form was related to its efficiency, but Lynn has tested this notion in the light of the results obtained in the General Certificate of Education by schools of different size.[27]

Lynn analysed the A-level examination results (1957) of 103 independent schools which took the examinations of the Oxford and Cambridge Joint Board, and of 76 maintained grammar schools in the county of London which take the London G.C.E. In both samples the largest schools obtained the best results in terms of passes per hundred pupils in the school, and especially so in terms of distinctions per hundred pupils in the school. (Girls do not benefit to the same extent as boys from school size: conceivably they respond less readily to a large school's instrumentality.) Analyses of the O-level results in the examinations of another G.C.E. board showed a similar though less pronounced trend. Lynn sums up his inquiry:

> The findings seem to show that... the small schools are not producing such good results as the large. They show also that this tendency becomes more marked with higher levels of academic attainment. The better achievements of large schools are most evident in university awards and are markedly present in distinctions at advanced level. In passes and failures at advanced and ordinary levels the differences are less striking.

Lynn speculates about the possible reasons for the superiority of large schools: perhaps they attract better teachers? In the case of the independent public schools, the most famous are large and may well attract the most talented teachers; but size, fame and attractiveness are less obviously associated in the case of maintained schools. Perhaps the large schools recruit more able pupils? Yet large schools and small schools do not differ much in their performance at O-level: they appear to have pupils of similar calibre. 'But two years later the children of the large schools are getting about 100 per cent more distinctions per 100 candidates at A-level.'

Large schools may be more stimulating, providing a more competitive atmosphere; but they are also likely to be more efficiently organized because the power of the headmaster can be used with greater effect. In the large school his power is greater in the Parsonian sense of capacity to mobilize resources for the attainment of organizational goals.

Blau has suggested how a leader's power increases with the number of his subordinates, essentially because he is able to spread the risk of defection:

The multiple supports of the power of a man who has the resources to command the compliance of one hundred others makes his power not only one hundred times as great but also immeasurably more secure than is the power of a man who only commands the compliance of one other. The basic reason is that power over many others enables a man to spread the risk of defections from his rule by taking into account the cost of such defections and insuring himself against their disadvantageous consequences.[28]

The staffroom of a large school will see the formation of opposition groups and protective alliances: mid-morning break is awaited with impatience for plotting the next move. But the chances of counter-opposition and the formation of loyalist cliques are also greater the larger the school; the probability of a number of sycophants increases. The large-school headmaster is unlikely to face total opposition:

> Besides, power over many others enables a man to use his power to bring those into line who might want to escape from his rule. Alternative supports make power independent of any one of them, and hence reinforce it far beyond their additive effect....[29]

But of even more importance is the greater manœuvrability that a headmaster of a large school has in deploying his staff. If he has only one mathematics master, he must use him with examination forms however weak he may be; but if he has five, he can use each where he is strongest. A 'qualified teacher' is still theoretically qualified to teach anything to anybody: this is a legal fiction which can lead to incompetence; but it legitimizes the power of the headmaster to deploy his staff as he thinks fit and is the basis of flexibility and efficiency when the school is large enough for the headmaster to take full advantage of it.

6 Participation and communication

Justice and efficiency are thought to be well served by 'participation' and communication. The truth is more complex. Both participation and communication in educational as well as industrial organizations may have unintended consequences. Participation often reduces the power of participants, and communication may impair their efficiency.

Headmasters have been slow to share their power. The morning assembly has all the ingredients of Athenian democracy; but in fact it is an occasion for the exercise of autocratic power. The headmaster's pronouncements are commands; it is unthinkable that they should be the subject of debate. The morning assembly is a confrontation and a show of strength. It is organized like a military parade and serves similar purposes. Staff solidarity is usually made manifest on the platform; and the head notes staff absences as signs of defection. This is an occasion for issuing orders, rewards and reprimands. Morning assemblies of the entire school are less common in boarding schools, where 'houses' make up a more genuinely plural society with competing centres of power. The day-school's morning assembly is a daily reaffirmation of highly centralized control.

The demand for 'participation' whether by pupils or staff has come later in schools than in industry. This is probably because their internal conflicts have been less acute and problematical. The industrial parallel has its uses, but can be seriously misleading. The conflict between workers and management is different in kind from the conflict between pupils and staff. While pupils may for some purposes be seen as 'lower-order participants' in the organization, they are also the organization's product. And they have many of the characteristics of the self-employed working under guidance for their own profit. They may wish to be different kinds of product or to achieve their finished character by other means; and therein lies the possibility of conflict. But their gain is not management's loss.

Pupils may be seen in various lights: as 'self-employed', as 'products', as 'clients', and even as 'patients'. In their character as 'patients', schools feel some obligation to retain and help them even when they prove 'inefficient' – indeed, some schools may feel a special obligation to retain them when they prove particularly inefficient. The criteria of membership applied by schools to pupils are different from those applied by factories and offices to employees. But this is not so with teachers. Their relationship with their superiors is an employer – employee relationship; they exchange their efficiency for pay and conditions of service. In their case there is a genuine bargain, a symmetrical relationship. They have been curiously laggard in requiring their terms of service to include an effective say in school-wide affairs. The reason may be in part that they have remarkable freedom in their conduct of classroom affairs. But the contrast with developments in industrial employment is striking.

The gain in efficiency to be expected from joint consultation was argued by Elton Mayo and his associates in the nineteen-thirties; and industry on both sides of the Atlantic paid some attention. Workers would perform better if they felt they belonged. Industrial strife, labour turnover and absenteeism might be cured through a sense of participation. In the postwar period experiments in industrial democracy multiplied; in Britain the John Lewis Partnership and the Glacier Metal Company are well-known examples.

Schools have remained comparatively undemocratized. In March 1970 it was possible for the headmaster of a Leicestershire 'Upper School' to write to the *Guardian* stating that he had disbanded the school council. The fact that an experiment in pupil democracy had met with little success is not perhaps surprising; what is remarkable is that the experiment was discontinued by the headmaster 'in a fit of pique or frustration'. A feature of the school organization with considerable symbolic if not functional importance was abandoned, apparently, without the need for ratification by parents, local education authorities, or staff. It was sufficient, in the headmaster's words, that 'I decided to put the clock back.'[1] University vice-chancellors and perhaps most managing directors would be powerless to modify their organizations in so summary a manner.

But headmasters are petty despots. They are not despots on the grand scale, because they have no voice in the major issues which concern their schools. In the maintained schools they have no say in matters of finance and resources and recruitment of personnel. They must take the children allocated to them, and often the staff. And of rather less significance, they have little or no discretion with regard to time off for themselves and their assistants for attending conferences and professional meetings held in school hours. The lack of some degree of freedom in the disposal of their time gives them sub-professional status.

The central argument of this book is that the power of schools should be expanded, and that such expansion is possible by increasing the power of both headmasters and assistants. This can be arranged without the increased power of one group or individual cancelling out the powers of others. Both the Plowden Report on primary schools and the Donnison Report on grammar schools envisaged and recommended such a general expansion of power. The fact that there is a maldistribution of power within schools should not lead us to the conclusion that they have too much. A better distribution of power can, in some circumstances, put more power into the system.

At present schools are underpowered because they are cut off from their social environment and have no authority to make decisions in relation to major environmental demands. In this they differ from industrial organizations whose managers must make great (and often risky) decisions about marketing different kinds of product, perhaps lengthening or shortening the production process, cutting the costs of production and cheapening their product. Headmasters (and their assistants), as managers of educational organizations, have no such power to make far-reaching decisions about the school's relationship to its social environment.

The major decisions of industrial managers are fiscal, relating, for example, to cutting costs and raising production. Analogous decisions in education are taken outside the schools.

In consequence the power of headmasters in maintained schools is comparatively trivialized. They are in much the same position as the managers of a French government monopoly described by Crozier: 'The managers of the Monopoly themselves are in a relatively inferior position, in that they are not competent to deal with what are normally the main considerations of managerial decision-making – the fiscal considerations.'[2] They have power only over secondary, internal issues.

Schools are instruments of social policy and it is inconceivable that headmasters will be given power over their 'input' and their 'output'. It is precisely because they have a measure of power over such matters that direct-grant schools are likely to disappear. But short of such extreme power, the Donnison Report recommends a general expansion of power within schools. The direct-grant schools which become maintained comprehensive schools will retain some of their characteristics, especially some freedom of financial manœuvre; and 'all schools doing similar work on a similar scale should have the same sort of autonomy that we recommend for former direct-grant schools'.[3] This would mean a considerable increase in power for many local authority schools, for, as the Donnison Report rightly observes: 'Maintained schools vary enormously in the degree of independence they have.'

There will be external control over the admission of pupils and over the number, qualifications and salaries of staff, but 'Within the general framework of public control, we think that the governors and the head should be left to run the school.'[4] Central and local government will approve financial estimates, but 'leave the school to decide on the order of priority between the various calls on their resources provided they keep within these estimates'. (The Plowden Report on primary schools makes similar, though more modest, recommendations relating to discretionary spending.[5]) In fact this is a far cry from the major fiscal decisions that industrial managers must make to maintain their organizations in their social environments; the notion that a school might decide to extend or contract its courses in response to its 'market' is unthinkable. But these proposals are a tribute to the principle that financial control is at the heart of managerial power.

Both the Plowden and Donnison Reports would increase the power of headteachers at the expense of the local education authority. The Plowden Report observes: 'There is a good deal of evidence that heads are sometimes ignored or by-passed by authorities where they clearly ought to have a say.'[6] The Donnison Report recommends that 'The school should be responsible for advertising for staff and appointing them, provided it keeps within the total establishment approved by the authority and observes minimum specifications about educational qualifications.' 'Thus the school, and the head in particular, should have the main say in deciding who should be appointed.' This would be a departure from current practice in many schools: 'This is not always the way in which maintained schools work at present.'[7]

Both reports make recommendations relating to time off. The Plowden Report says that 'headteachers should be allowed proper discretion in deciding the circumstances in which they themselves and members of their staffs may be occasionally absent from school'.[8] The Donnison Report correctly sees this as an issue of professional status: 'The heads and their teaching staff are professionals. Their knowledge, experience and status cannot be fully used unless it is acknowledged and respected.' Freedom to take time off to attend courses and conferences, without obtaining the permission of the local education authority, would be such an acknowledgement.[9]

Headteachers should have more power; so should their assistants. Neither report sees any inconsistency in such recommendations; nor is there any. Primary school headteachers who were questioned for the Plowden Report thought in the main that assistant teachers had sufficient freedom in the conduct of their work; 'a substantially smaller number' of assistant teachers thought they were consulted sufficiently about the running of the school. The report urges more consultation between head and assistant teachers, which is possible without the former's 'essential leadership being impaired'.[10] This consultation should relate to school-wide, and not simply classroom, affairs: 'assistant staff should be drawn as much as possible into the planning and organization of the school life'.

The Donnison Report likewise urges consultation – but with due regard for seniority and the primacy of the headmaster:

> The head (often in co-operation with the heads of other schools) must decide on academic matters – on what is taught and how it is taught – being guided by his teaching staff, current educational thinking, the advice of H.M. Inspectors and local education authority professional advisers. He should be responsible for the appointment and deployment of staff within the establishment approved by the authority, taking advantage of the advice and expertise available to him among local education authority officers, governors and his senior staff.[11]

Primary schools and secondary schools differ considerably in the way power is distributed within them. The primary school head is in some ways more powerful, less curtailed by the demands and expectations of his or her assistant staff, and less constrained by external, 'market' considerations (especially with the abolition of 'eleven-plus' tests). Blyth has made much of the 'autonomy' of the primary school,[12] which he ascribes to a variety of causes including the trust and forbearance of parents and the strong attachment to school found among children at this stage. Other sociologists have drawn a similar distinction between primary and secondary schools: 'Secondary school heads are often less free in respect of curriculum (specified in examination syllabi), and grouping procedures (determined by who shall prepare for given syllabi).'[13] This observation properly focuses attention on the autonomy of the headteacher rather than of the school in a more general sense.

Recent research into decision-making in primary schools and secondary schools of all types bears out this distinction. Sharma conducted inquiries in a stratified sample of schools to discover decision-making practices as reported and as desired by teachers. Teachers were questioned about actual and ideal practice on twenty-eight issues covering eleven major decision-areas in schools, namely, curriculum content; selection and purchase of teaching aids; selection, promotion and transfer of teachers; teaching responsibilities and other duties; pupil evaluation and guidance; pupil conduct; extra-curricular activities; school buildings and grounds; and public relations.[14] Teachers were asked who was usually involved in making decisions in these various areas, and who they thought should be involved.

The responses of teachers in different types of secondary school were substantially alike (except that teachers in secondary modern and comprehensive schools wished to participate more than grammar school teachers in decisions relating to discipline). They differed sharply from teachers in primary schools both in the practices they reported and desired. Secondary school teachers saw the head as being concerned (either alone or in consultation) with 60 per cent of the decision-making; primary teachers saw the head as being concerned with 75 per cent. And primary teachers saw the head as taking decisions on 54 per cent of the issues without consultation; secondary teachers saw the head as acting by himself on 39 per cent of the issues. The latter would wish him to take decisions by himself on only 14 per cent of the issues; but primary teachers were willing for the head to act alone on 29 per cent.

Neither secondary nor primary teachers wished the head to be involved in decisions over fewer issues; indeed, secondary school teachers wished him to be involved in more. But they required far more to be taken in consultation with assistant staff. (Neither group of teachers saw parents as having any significant place in decision-making.) They especially wished to see the head's powers extended at the expense of the local education authority: they thought he should have a voice in matters relating to school buildings and furnishings, and to school grounds.

Secondary school teachers, perhaps surprisingly, approved of the head taking decisions by himself over what is taught in the school; the rules of behaviour for pupils; how often parents and the public should be invited to school; and the programme of activities when parents and the public come. They wished to be consulted over the following matters which heads were seen as keeping to themselves: responsibility allowances; teachers' timetables; other duties of teachers; the selection of teaching aids; the frequency of examinations; the frequency of reports to parents; and the type of report form used. In short, they wished to extend the range of issues with which the headmaster is concerned; and they wished to be consulted over a larger number of issues; but they saw a number of key matters as being the headmaster's sole concern.

They apparently saw no inconsistency in enlarging the headmaster's decision-making activities and also their own.

The staff meeting is the formal machinery for consultation; it has symbolic as well as functional significance. Headmasters who call infrequent meetings may be thought to have lost their nerve; those who hold *ad hoc* meetings with sections of staff may be thought to conspire against the rest. The staff meeting has more subtle purposes than the making of decisions. The meeting of the entire staff is an expression of solidarity, even though it merely agrees with the decisions the head has already taken; but it is seldom seen as so important that it should run on after the end of the school day or be convened out of term.

The reports of the Clarendon Commission on the public schools (1864) and of the Taunton Commission on the endowed grammar schools (1868) both recommended formal staff meetings. Arnold had employed a system of regular and frequent staff consultation which had worked well. A senior member of the Rugby staff told the Clarendon Commission: 'It is attributable to that, that we have so very harmonious a working of the school.' Disharmony at Eton might be remedied by similar measures. The Commission felt that

> the want of regular meetings for consultation (at Eton), and of recognized opportunities for making suggestions and freely discussing them, has worked prejudicially on the relations of the assistants towards their head and towards each other, while it has probably retarded very much the progress of improvement in the school.

> Valuable suggestions and useful information which assistant masters, and they only, are qualified to afford, may be lost for want of a recognized opportunity of communicating them.

Both the Clarendon and the Taunton Commissions wanted headmasters to be stronger; the 'participation' of assistant masters was seen not as an impediment, but as an aid, to this end. But the staff meetings which were becoming a general feature of public school and grammar school organization in the second half of the nineteenth century did more than promote communication; they brought assistant masters into the school. Hitherto their role had been circumscribed, restricted to class teaching: they 'remained in a sense outside the school'.[15] Now they became responsible, along with the headmaster, for the school's 'tone'. Their obligations became more pervasive and diffuse. Hitherto they had turned out as curious spectators when their pupils had rioted, idle bystanders who left the headmaster to cope with such emergencies alone. When assistant masters were called in to help, they might do so as a favour, but not in the line of duty.[16] The staff meeting was a symptom of their incorporation and of the increasingly 'total' character of the public school environment for all its members.

We have no systematic evidence on the powers and procedures of contemporary staff meetings. Probably they have advanced little since the days of Thring. One research into boarding school education reports a headmaster as saying: 'I admit, I can't think of a decision (at a staff meeting) being made against my will.'[17] Procedures probably vary considerably; but the essentially consultative nature of the staff meeting is probably general. Staff meetings may be little more than briefings: the headmaster instructs his staff about his plan of campaign. It may also be the occasion for allocating non-routine jobs, for instance in connection with Sports Day or the school play. End-of-term and end-of-year meetings see assistant staff rendering an account of themselves and of their pupils' progress. More 'constitutional' and genuinely participatory government has been imposed on colleges of education by the Weaver Report.[18] A genuine sharing of power in schools may similarly need to be imposed from above. In the meantime headmasters tend to argue, 'I have the responsibility; I must have the power.'

An influential model is university government, at least in the somewhat idealized version presented by Ashby. According to this model:

> The government and organization of British universities is a remarkable phenomenon, quite unlike government in industry or civil service or the church; for policy is not dictated from above and there is no descending chain of responsibility and

authority.... University government is a sort of inverted hierarchy.... Policy-making begins – in a healthy university at any rate – at the level of departments, among the teaching staff. It then rises to the level of the faculty, where conflicting proposals from departments are reconciled in the presence of representatives of all teachers of the faculty. From the faculty it goes to the Senate....[19]

By and large it is true to say that the main direction of flow of new ideas and proposals is from below upwards and not in the reverse direction.[20]

This picture does not square with the perceptions of most academics. Recent inquiries by Halsey and Trow reveal 'widespread discontent' among English academics with the power-structure of their universities. More than 80 per cent of academic staff below the level of professor see the university as a professorial oligarchy. This inquiry, which was carried out with more than twelve hundred university staff, produced 'evidence of considerable discontent with the present system, and of support even for very sweeping changes among surprisingly high numbers of teachers'.[21]

The power of professors may in fact protect junior members of staff from the power of administrators. Universities, colleges, and schools (except the very smallest) are hybrid organizations: there is a built-in conflict between those who wholly or mainly administer the organization, and those who wholly or mainly teach or research. The power struggle of the future in British universities is likely to be more openly between academics and vice-chancellors, rather than between professors and their junior colleagues. In universities and colleges the confrontation (and perhaps resolution) will occur formally on senates; in schools at staff meetings. Senates and staff meetings bring together two opposed social systems which rest on different principles of action.

The problem is not to bring these two systems together, but to keep them apart. The extent of their interaction probably needs to vary with the phases in the life-history of a school. When a school is founded, or when it embarks on some major innovation, the two sides will often come together. The administrators are not yet administering uniform events. The intense interaction at the inception of a secondary school has been described in the following terms:

> there was much meeting and discussion, during which the Head was able to establish his prime right to decision-making, but in which all the staff felt they were involved in the important decisions. In the course of this, strongly shared norms and values developed as the group worked enthusiastically towards a common endeavour.[22]

But within a relatively short space of time the head became 'bureaucratized': he withdrew from communication and the frequency of staff meetings declined.

The author of the research report deplores this change; but it may be a natural and appropriate progression of events. In all educational institutions but the very smallest two- or three-teacher schools, two distinctive decision-making systems emerge: one is within or closely related to the teaching situation and involves on-the-job improvisation, dealing with unique events and personalities, calling for the application of 'particularistic' criteria in reaching decisions; the other concerns the regularities of system-wide behaviour, the ordering of uniform events, and the application of 'universalistic' criteria to decision-making. Litwak has argued that such organizations call for 'mechanisms of segregation': 'These permit mutually antagonistic social forms to exist side by side in the same organization without ruinous friction.'[23]

The two styles of communication, consultation and participation are appropriate to their respective spheres of action. Teachers dealing with day-to-day classroom matters and relatively short-term teaching and curricular problems are frequently in an ambiguous situation which general rules do not fit; they need the emotional support which comes from frequent discussion and consultation with equal colleagues, and this is available in the staffroom at intervals throughout the day. The contacts they require are informal, frequent and highly personal. They are dealing with situations in which general rules are of little help.

There are other problems in schools relating to long-term curriculum planning, the formulation of general rules of conduct and the like which call for a different decision-making style:

infrequent meetings, formal, hierarchical and impersonal in their conduct. The implementation and enforcement of such decisions calls for the 'formalistic impersonality' of classical, Weberian bureaucracy. The other sphere does not.[24]

Joan Woodward in her industrial studies has highlighted very similarly contrasted decision-making systems and has examined their bearing on the amount and flow of communication. In unit production the communications system must often bring people together, from day to day; but in mass production 'such a system might well reduce efficiency'. And she concludes: 'Communications systems cannot be good or bad in themselves; they are good only if they link people together in such a way as to further the objectives of the firm.'[25] Similarly in schools: if frequent, formal staff meetings are necessary, this probably means that the informal system of the staffroom is not working adequately, and that the formal apparatus of 'universalistic' rules may be applied disastrously to 'particularistic' schoolboy problems.

Frequent memoranda from superiors, and house journals, give an appearance of 'participation' when there may be little in reality. And congested notice boards bear witness to a surfeit of information which, from its very amount, defeats its purpose. Modern organizations are in danger of doing so much communicating that they have neither time nor energy for anything else. The urgent need in schools, colleges and universities today is the radical reduction of communication. To receive information from a higher office may be irrelevant to one's job but crucial to one's status. Distribution lists signal status dispositions. Teachers commonly complain that when the headmaster has important information to impart, the man to ask is the caretaker. Their complaint recognizes the distribution of information as a status-conferring (or subverting) device. Its contribution to efficiency in work may be comparatively trivial.

Teachers, then, would like more say in the way schools are run. This is true of both secondary and primary teachers; but the latter see the head as wielding more power and would be prepared to have more in his hands. Assistant teachers would by no means denude headteachers of power; but they would not admit parents to any and would substantially reduce that of local education authorities. But headteachers exercise power within very circumscribed limits, for they take no fiscal decisions, which are usually the basis of effective managerial power. While deploring heads who communicate little and hold staff meetings infrequently, teachers nevertheless seem to recognize that there are relatively distinct styles and spheres of decision-making; and that policy in its more general form, regarding curriculum and school rules, is primarily the concern of the head. Schools, like other large institutions dealing essentially in social behaviour, are organizational hybrids; and the answer to their problems of internal conflict is not to pretend that they are not, but to explore the minimum workable amounts of participation and communication between teachers and their more bureaucratized superiors.

Bureaucratized superiors in schools, colleges and universities may feel they have more to gain from participation with pupils and students. They would probably be right. And this is the danger of 'student power': if it is in fact plebiscitary power, it may seriously weaken the power of intermediate ranks and give preponderant power to the summit.

Schoolboys, like their teachers, were brought into the school in the middle of the nineteenth century; and in the process they lost the considerable measure of autonomy they had hitherto enjoyed. School councils have not restored them to their former state.

The eighteenth-century public school has been described as an enormous society of boys between the ages of eight and eighteen, governed by an unwritten code of its own making, an almost free republic of 100, 200 or 500 members.[26] The traditional view was that outside lessons schoolboys had the right to freedom from adult control. A boy had to attend at meals, prayers, classes and bedtime; otherwise he could go where he liked and do as he pleased.

> As a result of their freedom over many years, Victorian youth in all the public schools inherited a code of rights covering the use of its leisure, whether it was in sports or games, fighting, fishing, hunting, fagging or dramatics. Both juniors and prefects defended these rights against all comers, even the headmaster....[27]

The schoolboy rebellions at Eton, Harrow and Rugby in the late eighteenth and early nineteenth centuries occurred when these ancient rights appeared to be threatened. Rugby rebelled against Tait's attempt to modify school bounds; Harrow rebelled against Butler, who had questioned the right of monitors to cane juniors at will. 'Ironically enough, the school supported the monitors. There was a general strike, and seven monitors were ultimately expelled.'[28]

When schoolmasters do not control schoolboys, schoolboys do – but usually more repressively. This has been observed in contemporary progressive schools: 'the social controls and limits on freedom may be as great or even greater from being the enforced norms of the informal organization – that is the children – as from being laid down from above by adults in a public school.'[29] In other words, the bully takes over. This is the other side of the coin of schoolboy autonomy.

It was a prominent side until the eighteen-sixties, and apparently out of respect for the tradition of schoolboy informal self-government, headmasters were reluctant to interfere. Brutality among the boys in the Long Chamber at Eton in the eighteen-forties was notorious, but 'Even the headmaster of the time, Dr Hawtrey, himself a most humane man, made no attempt to investigate, so strong was the convention that boys must rule themselves.'[30] George Moberly, headmaster of Winchester in the middle of the century, refused to be informed of schoolboy bullying and brutality – again, apparently, out of a sensitive regard for traditions of schoolboy autonomy.[31]

The new-style self-government was to take the form of shared authority, within the boundary of the school's formal organization; and its instrument was to be the school council. This form of pupil power was pioneered in the progressive schools; subsequently it received widespread support in American high schools; and at present is being tried out, rather gingerly, in many English maintained secondary schools. It has been generally disappointing to all concerned; but probably no more disappointing than similar participatory schemes for workers in industry.

School councils vary considerably in their composition and powers; in the main they give advice to the headmaster, which he may or may not take. In a few extreme cases they are legislative bodies, enacting rules for the entire school, which are binding on staff and pupils alike. Twentieth-century wars fought in the name of democracy have given them a considerable fillip. The nineteen-twenties were their heyday: the progressive schools founded earlier like Bedales (1893) and Abbotsholme (1889) were more cautious and conservative in the democratic powers they accorded to pupils. Abbotsholme was established by Cecil Reddie to educate the future 'directing classes' and at first had a rather traditional prefect system until Sharp transformed it into the Reds' Council in the nineteen-thirties. Even after its transformation its purpose was to spread ideas and suggestions, not to make rules or policy: to improve the quality of the life of the school, and not to regulate it. At Bedales the school council has not been prominent; it is intended to give a training in individual self-discipline, rather than a general practice of self-government. Pupil-participation at Leighton Park (1890) has similarly been somewhat muted. The school council consists of two elected members from each form, two staff representatives, and the headmaster is president. It can discuss any subject affecting the life of the school, but it has no legislative authority. It does not make school rules and has no disciplinary powers.

After the First World War school democracy took courage (indeed, it did so during the war under Homer Lane at his reformatory, the 'Little Commonwealth'). Neill founded Summerhill in England in 1924; Curry Dartington Hall in 1925 (the same year that Frensham Heights was founded); and Bertrand and Dora Russell founded Beacon Hill in 1927. Curry was more cautious about democracy than either Neill or the Russells. At first he set up a 'headmaster's advisory council' which consisted of six elected senior pupils who had informal discussions with the head on the running of the school; later this was enlarged but styled the 'moot' to underline its essentially advisory function.

Neill went to the extreme by Athenian democracy: rule by a full school meeting. Very few matters are outside its competence – only the appointment and dismissal of staff and the payment of bills. This 'parliament' meets weekly and can deal with all school rules, academic and curricular matters, the punishment of individuals, and the school's domestic arrangements.

At Beacon Hill Bertrand and Dora Russell established a school council which included all pupils and members of staff and other adults in the school such as the gardener and cook. The chairman was a pupil elected for a term, and it was his responsibility to call meetings of the council. Rules for the school were discussed and agreed to by vote; but, since few sanctions were imposed on those who broke the rules, a great deal of time was spent trying to arrive at rules which people were likely to keep.

Such experiments in the democratic government of schools have been initiated partly in the name of democracy, but primarily in the name of personal development. In America 'training for democracy' has been the over-riding purpose of pupil participation, at least in the theoretical literature on the subject. A survey of more than five hundred principals has shown that the main activity of councils in American high schools relates to extra-curricular activites: dances, parties, picnics and carnivals.[32] In the main the American councils cannot make or enforce rules: they are essentially advisory bodies.

A recent English study has concerned itself with the composition, powers and effectiveness of the school council at Abbotsholme; a northern boys' boarding school, Woodhouse Grove; a Yorkshire maintained grammar school, Keighley; and, for comparative purposes, a large American high school at Shawnee, Kansas City.[33] In all four schools the council is essentially advisory; in all four schools an overwhelming majority answered 'No' to the question: 'Do you think the school council has sufficient power or authority to be effective?' (The percentages were: Woodhouse Grove 66; Keighley 66; Abbotsholme 49; Kansas City 85.) But this mattered more to pupils at Abbotsholme and Woodhouse Grove:

> In the two boarding schools there was greater involvement and active participation, greater perception of the council's role, higher levels of knowledge and recall (of its activities), and a greater desire for the council to be successful. In the day schools there was less involvement; the council was seen as a less important aspect of the school, it tended to deal with more limited matters, and there were more criticisms of different aspects. It appears to be easier to establish councils, and obtain involvement in them, in community or boarding schools.[34]

The question was put to pupils in all four schools: 'Do you

generally regard the school council as a successful body?' Only 31 per cent at Woodhouse Grove said 'No', 35 per cent at Abbotsholme, but 64 per cent at Keighley and 57 per cent at Kansas City. To the question: 'Do you think the council gives pupils an effective say in school affairs?' 53 per cent said 'No' at Woodhouse Grove, 58 per cent at Abbotsholme, but 67 per cent at Keighley and 70 per cent at Kansas City. The most common reason for saying 'No' was that the head and staff control debate. (Nevertheless, even with such limitations, many English pupils appreciated the chance to speak impersonally to the head and senior staff and to raise issues that might in any other context have appeared impertinent.[35])

There was far deeper disenchantment with pupil-participation at Kansas City than in the English schools – conceivably because Americans expect more of their democratic institutions.

> Over half the sample state that the congress is a pseudo-democracy, with real power belonging to the principal and the faculty, and the result of pretending to share power with pupils is frustration with the working of the congress and alienation from the school. Again, well over a third of the pupils believe that the principal and faculty representatives control the debate and decisions, and use the congress as a means of controlling the school.[36]

Worker-participation in industry, like pupil-participation in schools, has often appeared bogus and a farce. The usual limitation of participation to consultation may be one reason for this – although the line between 'merely advising' and sharing in policy-making is not a firm one. Elliott Jaques has given an account of the difficulties and ambiguities of moving towards a genuinely policy-making Works Council at the Glacier Metal Company.[37] Participants themselves were uncertain whether the Works Council (1949) solely advised or made policy; but in any case, if the Council was not unanimous, management had the power to act.[38] Democracy in industry and schools has often seemed timid and ineffectual. Disappointment may arise from the assumption that democracy in an organization and a nation can be strictly comparable. At the national level participation may take the form of radical dissent; but participatory democracy in formal organizations is more often conservative and unadventurous. Participants must live and work alongside each other after some have pushed through measures which others strongly dislike. In a nation elected representatives have more fleeting relationships with the people affected by their measures; they need not live daily, perhaps hourly, with reproach.

Industrial democracy does not appear to have brought more power to industrial organization through a sense of belonging and stronger commitment by workers to its goals; but it often appears to have given more power to managers *vis-à-vis* the managed. The John Lewis Partnership is committed to sharing both profits and power. A careful attempt to evaluate these provisions shows that the workers are generally satisfied with the profit-sharing scheme; but only a minority of workers appear to be more favourably disposed towards the firm because of the complex representative system which emphasizes the accountability of the managers to the managed:

> But even this minority continue to view their immediate job interests in much the same fashion as the majority of rank and file Partners; in this respect, involvement in the Partnership system has no particular influence on their attitudes. Hence our conclusion that the ethos of the employment relationship for the non-managerial employees of the Partnership closely resembles that to be found in employing organizations of the usual kind. Although they may regard the Partnership as a 'good' employer, their relationship with it remains a 'calculative' rather than a 'normative' one; except for a small minority it does not entail any firm commitment to the Partnership's ideology.[39]

The elaborate systems of internal communication and of representation have not given workers power. 'Rather do they constitute a means of reinforcing the power of management over the managed.'[40] Participation may have the effect of limiting the power of participants, restricting their freedom of action. As Crozier has pointed out in his examination of French bureaucracy, 'lower participants' are learning to be very cautious of participation:

> It is far easier to preserve one's independence and integrity if one does not participate in decision-making.

If one accepts participation, one is bound to co-operate, i.e., to bear one's co-participants' pressure whether they are one's equals or one's superiors. People therefore rarely agree to participate without some substantial counterpart. They try to negotiate about their participation, and give it only if they feel that they will be adequately rewarded.[41]

The danger with involving lower participants in decisions about the running of schools, factories or universities is that the power of top managers is strengthened, and that of middle managers curtailed. As Jaques reports of the Glacier Metal Company, 'The consultative machinery came to be used as an executive by-passing mechanism.'[42] Pupil- and student-participation can be a form of 'plebiscitarianism' as dangerous as the opinion polls of resident social scientists, which enable top administrators to tell the organization what it (really) thinks. Appeals to student opinion may be a means of subverting staff power; they confer the legitimacy of seemingly democratic procedure. Housemasters, heads of department, professors, rank-and-file teachers, make up a plural society which is the major safeguard against unbridled autocracy. They may be especially adept at safeguarding their own particular statuses and privileges; but each keeps an eye on the pretensions of others. Participation by all ranks can too easily mean the diminished importance of intermediate centres of power and still further increases in the power of the highest.[43]

Responsibility is properly linked with power. Pupils are members of a school in a different sense and on different terms from their teachers. To be responsible is to be liable to punishment if things go wrong; pupils cannot be punished like their teachers for the failure of school policies, even if they had a hand in shaping them. Their claim to a share in power is weak. And the claim of headmasters to supreme power because theirs is the supreme responsibility, is also weaker than is commonly assumed. Teaching at all levels, and perhaps especially the highest, is a secure job, and punishment for failure rarely takes the form of dismissal or even demotion. The severest punishment will probably be the censure of superiors. And no one is quite sure what failure is – short of total breakdown of school discipline. Punishment usually takes the form of blockages to further promotion. Headmasters by definition are the promoted: they can come to less harm for their mistakes than their junior staff, unless they are under forty and looking for a bigger job. The strongest claimant to participant power is the young and talented teacher who still has a long way to go.

7 The advantages of bureaucracy

The development of bureaucracy over the past century has made us a less servile people. It has helped to make jobs secure and has based appointments and promotions on qualifications rather than personal connections. It has regulated activity through rules; but obedience to rules is probably less humiliating than submission to persons. The whim and caprice of superiors at work have been constrained. The advantages of these bureaucratic advances are nowhere more evident than in education. Abject governesses in private households have been succeeded by self-confident and self-respecting schoolmistresses in comprehensive schools. The gain in human dignity is incalculable. Assistant masters no longer risk dismissal when a new headmaster is appointed, as they did even at the turn of the century. Servility doubtless survives in schools (especially, perhaps, in private schools). It is unnecessary, irrelevant and dysfunctional.

Bureaucracies co-ordinate the diverse activities of specialists and organize them in a rational plan. They enjoin disciplined and predictable behaviour. Max Weber described the 'ideal-type' bureaucracy. Its essential characteristics are five in number: there is a clear-cut division of labour, and regular activities 'are distributed in a fixed way as official duties'; the organization is hierarchical, 'each lower office is under the control and supervision of a higher one'; there is a system of rules, and operations are governed by 'the application of these rules to particular cases'; the conduct of officials is impersonal, and duties are performed 'without hatred or passion, and hence without affection or enthusiasm'; and employment is based on technical qualifications, it is protected against arbitrary dismissal, and it 'constitutes a career. There is a system of promotions according to seniority or to achievement, or both.'[1]

Max Weber's account of bureaucratic organization has received close critical scrutiny and has been put to some empirical test. The original 'dimensions' of bureaucracy have been refined and elaborated. But most important of all are the clear indications in recent research that the various aspects of bureaucracy are relatively independent: organizations may, for example, have a well-defined system of rules without being particularly hierarchical, or may emphasize technical competence without placing stress on either specialization or impersonality of official conduct. A study of ten American organizations showed that there was very little correlation among the various classical dimensions of bureaucracy.[2]

An English study of fifty-two work organizations has led to a similar conclusion. This study indicates that the dimensions themselves require redefinition, and are probably four in number: 'the structure of activity' (embracing formalization and specialization); 'concentration of authority' (embracing centralization and organizational autonomy); 'line control of workflow' (embracing rules of job performance and promotion procedures); and 'relative size of supportive component' (embracing percentage of clerks and other supporting personnel). 'As a result of this dimensional analysis, it is clear that to talk in terms of the bureaucratic ideal type is not adequate, since the structure of an organization may vary along any of these four empirical dimensions'.[3]

This research into contemporary organizations is important not least because it enables us to look realistically at bureaucratization as a historical development. We need not expect to find all aspects of bureaucracy changing together and in unison. Thus we do not necessarily expect that a more hierarchical organization of education automatically goes hand-in-hand with greater centralization. Indeed, a close examination of changes in the organization of the education service in general and of schools in particular over the past hundred years shows these bureaucratic features in complete disarray; while some march forward steadily, others retreat. The most steady advance since the later nineteenth century probably relates to the employment of teachers on the basis of technical qualifications, protected against arbitrary dismissal, and constituting a career. Centralization, on the other hand, shows a more complicated pattern of advance and retreat.

The second half of the nineteenth century saw the rapid spread of many features of bureaucracy in industry and commerce, the army, the civil service, and education. A common feature of developments in all these spheres was the rationalization of appointment and promotion procedures, the redefinition and delimitation of jobs, and the establishment of hierarchical pyramids of command. In the world of industry and commerce such changes stemmed from the Companies Act of 1862: in the last thirty years of the century private enterprises were extensively converted into public companies run not by a family but by a board of directors. This development replaced the entrepreneur by 'a collectivity finding safety in rules and records. The profession of accountancy acquired a totally new importance. . . .'[4] But this rationalized and depersonalized new order 'also provided some antidote to the evil of nepotism, where wealth descended to heirs in the form of a factory which they were personally unfitted to run'.[5] Bureaucracy served equally the causes of justice and efficiency.

Cardwell's reform of the army in the same period had similar consequences. He succeeded in abolishing the purchase of commissions and promotions; but perhaps of greater importance was the centralization of power and its hierarchical ordering. Jobs in the higher levels of the War Department were redefined; the commander-in-chief was given greatly increased powers and responsibilities; and the right of appointing officers in the militia, which had hitherto been exercised by the lords-lieutenant of counties, was now transferred to the War Office. But probably the most important bureaucratic change, from the point of view of administrative efficiency, was the redefinition of the power and authority of the adjutant-general and the quartermaster-general. The latter was subordinated to the former.[6] Hitherto a dualism had existed similar to the dualism of headmaster and usher in the endowed schools, which will be discussed later in this chapter. When two officers are of co-equal and rival authority, the power of the organization is not increased, but considerably diminished. Due subordination of one to the other in an hierarchical system prevents the power of one being used to nullify the power of the other.

The bureaucratization of the civil service has probably done more for the dignity and self-respect of British intellectuals than any other institutional change of the past century. Noel Annan has described the Northcote–Trevelyan Report of 1853, which recommended entry into the civil service by open competitive examination, as the Bill of Rights of the intellectuals; and the implementation of the proposals, in the eighteen-seventies, as their Glorious Revolution: it was then ordained that men of good intellect should prosper.[7] Influential contemporaries saw these changes as conferring too much dignity for too little service: 'The object, in point of fact, is to turn the sixteen thousand places in the civil service of this empire into so many exhibitions for poor scholars.'[8]

Along with the changed mode of recruitment to the civil service went its restructuring along hierarchical lines. Previously undifferentiated jobs were now placed in divisions or grades according to their actual importance and power. The Playfair Commission of 1875 recommended the identification and due subordination of subordinates: 'We are satisfied that in many, if not most offices, there is too large a proportion of clerks, all presumed to be doing the same work, and to be entitled to promotion to the highest clerkships, whilst as a matter of fact many of them are, and must be, employed on routine work.'[9] A small upper division and large lower division were therefore recommended – a pyramid of power based on the realistic definition of jobs.

The education service served these new bureaucracies by certificating its own products and grading them for appropriate levels of bureaucratic employment. In organizing itself for this task it bureaucratized itself. The development of a system of public examinations for schools, which began with the Oxford and Cambridge 'Locals' in 1858, was in effect the certification of a peripatetic (and therefore self-respecting) élite for recruitment to bureaucratic offices.[10] Under the terms of the Public Schools Act of 1868 and the Endowed Schools Act of 1869 the public schools and the grammar schools rationalized their organization, defined more closely different levels of power and authority, and standardized their procedures in the interest of producing a standardized product.

And they provided careers no longer characterized by extremes of humiliation and subservience.

The non-bureaucratic teacher par excellence was the private tutor. His condition was abject. Usually on a level with the menial servants of the household, he was equally at the mercy of his employers, and 'we must expect the servile station agreeable only to a low and grovelling disposition'. This was the view of James Barclay, voiced in a *Treatise on Education* which he published in 1743. There are virtually no dissenting views in the eighteenth century. Locke had expected much of the private tutor, especially as a man of worldly experience and independent bearing; but few writers on the subject thought such dignity possible. Swift in his *Essay on Education* described and deplored the tutor's dependence on the pupil's mother; a century later Joseph Priestley,[11] George Chapman[12] and David Williams wrote from personal experience of the humiliations endured by scholars of distinction who were obliged to take up private tutoring. 'A man who is to form a gentleman by his example and his instruction,' wrote Williams, 'should be totally independent of parents who are his inferiors in accomplishments. I never saw a private tutor, under the eye and direction of a great man, without the marks of a dependant; and more likely to injure his pupil by his spirit and manners, than to improve them by his instructions.'[13] Private tutors could only be described as 'the most servile and accommodating order in the community'.[14]

The servility of the tutor was exceeded only by that of the governess. She has been vividly portrayed in contemporary fiction. Clara Mordaunt, the heroine of Lady Blessington's novel, *The Governess*, published in 1839, endured a condition similar to Charlotte Brontë at the Sidgwicks. 'As for correcting [the children],' wrote Charlotte to her sister, 'I quickly found that was out of the question; they are to do as they like. A complaint to the mother only brings black looks on myself, and unjust, partial excuses to screen the children.'[15] The insecurity and degradation of governesses have been abundantly described: 'their fate may be at the pleasure of their employers; they may be seldom suffered to have a will or opinion; and they may be held in a state of servility as unprofitable as it is wretched.'[16] Salvation came only in the second half of the nineteenth century through formal qualifications which gained for them employment in the expanding system of bureaucratized schools.

Before this time both schools and universities were quasi-bureaucracies, providing a loose organizational structure within which semi-independent practitioners operated. The allegiance of teachers and university tutors was more to their clients than to their organization. Indeed, the greater part of their income was often from clients rather than their organization, in the form of fees, presents and even tips. Semi-independence of the school or college organization is one side of the picture; the other is ingratiation with pupils and their parents in the hope of a generous gratuity.

The headmaster of Eton had many of the characteristics of a head waiter until his position and salary were redefined and regularized after the report of the Clarendon Commission in 1864. In 1763 he received £411 in tips from his pupils and their parents. Annual gratuities were not obligatory, but parents saw the advantage of 'plentifully greasing the headmaster's palm'.[17] The Clarendon Commission found him in receipt of a gross income in excess of £6,000; his net income, after paying his eighteen assistants out of his own pocket, was £4,500. His statutory emoluments were only £375 per annum (and a rent-free house); he was making a further £5,700 from entrance fees, leaving presents, and annual payments by the boys. The commissioners recommended that he should have a fixed income of £4,000 per annum.

Until the later nineteenth century schools and colleges had members of staff incorporated and attached with widely varying degrees of commitment and obligation. Headmasters and other masters on the foundation were often virtually part-time appointments. John James, headmaster of Oundle from 1809 to 1829, received an income of £60 per annum from the foundation; his income as curate of Oundle was £70 per annum. Extra subjects not prescribed by the foundation were taught by 'extra masters' who often made a good income from the fees they charged but were not incorporated in the school and had no position in the formal hierarchy. Foundation masters, who were usually paid to teach classical subjects, might also teach 'extra subjects', and charged fees for doing so. Some headmasters appear to have done nothing else. For a considerable portion of their time, or even for all of it, staff worked as private, fee-paid tutors as distinct from salaried employees of the organization. Carlisle's inquiry (1818) into the condition of endowed grammar schools discovered that the headmaster of Bampton Grammar School in Oxfordshire, for example, had not been into the school to teach for the past ten or fifteen years. The headmaster of the grammar school at Mansfield similarly taught no foundation scholars.[18] 'Every single minute of duty, or item of equipment, not laid down in the contract was carefully noted.... Even a headmaster like Arnold did not despise the private student.'[19]

It was possible for virtually autonomous, private enterprise departments to be established within the framework of a school's general organization. Stephen Hawtrey established a private enterprise mathematics department at Eton in 1837. He obtained a forty-year lease on a site in the college, built his own mathematical school in the form of a rotunda, a lecture-theatre which would accommodate 350 pupils, and recruited his own assistant mathematical masters. In 1851, after fourteen years in this endeavour, he persuaded the college authorities to make mathematics a compulsory subject (three hours a week). But he had been at Eton for nineteen years before he was officially recognized as a member of staff. His assistant mathematical masters never were.[20]

Part-time commitment to their official duties was common among professors at Oxford and Cambridge in the middle of the nineteenth century. The stipends attached to professorships – like the emoluments of many headmasters – were insufficient in themselves. Giving evidence to the Royal Commission on Cambridge in 1852 Sir Henry Maine observed: 'It is virtually impossible that a professor should make the conduct of his faculty the principal occupation of his life. I myself am a practising barrister – my two immediate predecessors were beneficed clergymen.'[21]

Many tutors both at public schools and at the ancient universities, had a tenuous and ambiguous relationship with the school or college. They were not simply semi-detached; they were wholly detached. They were fee-paid employees of students, and entirely outside the jurisdiction of the school or college. The tutorial system at Eton evolved from a practice of purely private tutoring by non-college personnel: 'In early days it was no uncommon thing for the sons of the great to bring with them to school a private tutor of their own.'[22]

In the later eighteenth century there were severe critics of this apparently widespread practice. Thomas Sheridan pointed out that such tutors simply did the boy's exercises for him and assisted him 'in construing the lesson appointed for the next day'.[23] Vicesimus Knox, headmaster of Tonbridge School, was more forthright in his condemnation:

> It has indeed been the custom among the richer orders to combine the advantage of a public and private education, by placing their sons at a celebrated school, and at the same time under the care of a private tutor, resident in the school or in its neighbourhood. The business of the private tutor is often, in this case, little more than to make the boy's exercises for him.... A private tutor, whose sole employment consists in removing the difficulties attending the discipline of a great school, is unintentionally the promoter of idleness, and consequently of ignorance, vice and misery.[24]

The distinguishing feature of bureaucratic employment is a salary paid by the employing organization, as distinct from a fee paid directly to the practitioner by a client. An uneasy compromise between pre-bureaucratic and bureaucratic employment was evident at Eton as late as 1862, when the Royal Commission on the Public Schools was holding its inquiries. 'Extra teaching' was still given; the tutors were employees of the college; but the extent of such teaching and the amount paid for it was determined by private agreement with the parents. One Eton teacher described his practice: 'I simply leave it to the parents.... I take simply what is given to me.'[25]

The bureaucratization of Oxford and Cambridge college tutors does not appear to have occurred until the early nineteenth century. Before this time a successful college fellow might attract numerous and wealthy students and so attain a position of considerable independence. His less successful colleagues were equally at the mercy of college and clients. At St John's College, Cambridge, in 1565, there were forty-seven fellows of whom five were without pupils. Mostly they had three or four; some had as many as fifteen. John Preston of Queen's College, had sixteen fellow-commoners and was referred to with some envy as 'the greatest pupil-monger in England in man's memory, having 16 fellow-commoners (most heirs to fair estates) admitted in one year at Queen's College'.[26] In its organization and discipline a college resembled an inn of court:

> The tutorial system was totally different [in the sixteenth century] from that which now prevails. A parent on bringing his son made his own choice of a tutor; the tutor undertook to look after the finances, the conduct, and the reading of the pupil, and stood to him *in loco parentis*; the fees were a matter of private agreement. From the outside point of view, the college was little more than a collection of 'coaches', who lived and compelld their charges to live under one roof. A minor result of the system, which is not without its bearing on the fortunes of the college, was that Fellows with a large connection were relatively independent of the Master and their colleagues; for they could always meet a threat of punishment for breaches of discipline with the counter-threat that they would carry off their clientele.[27]

Today the academic who has obtained large research funds from external sources may be in a similar position of power.

At Balliol the change to the present-day bureaucratic form of employment and organization was occurring in the later eighteenth century.

> In 1772–1773 the accounts show the payments of relatively substantial sums to three Fellows, presumably for tuition, for from 1780 the Fellows to whom such payments were made are called *tutores*. There is nothing in the Register to explain this innovation, but it may represent the change-over from the Elizabethan system of private arrangements between tutor and pupil (or his parents) to something like the nineteenth-century system of college tutors.[28]

The position of professors – especially underpaid Regius professors – in the Scottish universities in the early nineteenth century well illustrates the problems and indignities attendant in pre-bureaucratic academic employment. The pre-bureaucratic professor was an entrepreneur who fought rival teachers of his own subject as dangerous competitors and resisted the development of subjects closely allied to his own, and the recognition of new subjects for graduation. At Glasgow college professors received an average of £300 per annum, Regius professors £50.

> The greater part of a professor's income was often derived from class and examination fees which depended on the number of students. Clearly professors of recognized subjects enrolled large numbers of students, and were well paid in comparison with those in fringe disciplines. . . . Personal interests were frequently hostile to change and encouraged recognized teachers to form conservative groupings, keen to preserve their status and monopoly.[29]

Private teachers attracted students from university professors by offering more attractive courses and charging lower fees. The universities had ill-defined organizational boundaries, affording inadequate shelter for their members, who were obliged strenuously to fend for themselves. The struggle for survival has been vividly told in the case of Thomas Charles Hope, Professor of Chemistry and Medicine at Edinburgh from 1799 to 1834. The University provided him with little more than a title, and,

> like some of his medical colleagues at Edinburgh, [he] received neither salary nor capital and running expenses which he therefore met himself. Clearly he was heavily reliant on the fees paid by members of his class. An unsalaried professor like Hope depended on the financial rewards of gaining popularity with a large number of students. . . . For many years Hope's emoluments were the highest received by a professor in a Scottish university, his remuneration from class fees hovering around £2,000 a year. Given this sort of financial independence it is not surprising that professors tended to be monopolistic, jealously guarding their disciplines against both internal and external competition. Hope was no exception in this regard: he allowed his tutorial assistant to use his apparatus for explanation but not for demonstration; and he regarded the proposal made by the Scottish Universities Commission [1826], that medical students

could attend private teachers for an imperative second course of chemistry, as a condemnation of his efficiency as well as an attack on his professorial rights.[30]

The independence of a fee-income is one side of the coin; the other, as a contemporary pointed out in 1830 in the *Quarterly Review*, is that such a professor 'is forced to become a commercial speculator, and under the dead weight of its degrading influence, his original researches are either neglected or abandoned.'[31]

The bureaucratization of schools has given more dignity and power to headmasters; and it has given more to assistant masters. There is no paradox in this, unless we subscribe to a 'zero-sum' notion of power, which would lead us to expect that one status group could increase its power only at the expense of another. Headmasters have gained power as co-ordinators of ever more diverse activities in ever larger organizations; and especially they have gained power from the hierarchical ordering of their staff. Assistant masters have gained power through improved academic qualifications and security of tenure. They are no longer employed and paid by a man, but by an organization.

The precondition of headmasterly power was the dethronement of the usher. Between the fourteenth and the nineteenth centuries he had achieved such a position of strength that he could effectively thwart the intentions of the head. The usher was variously styled: under-master at Westminster, sub-master at St Paul's, second master at Charterhouse; but whatever his title, the foundation statutes usually left no doubt about his subordinate rank. His income from the foundation ranged from about a half of the headmaster's (as at Giggleswick) to a third (as at Oundle). The Public Schools Commission (1864) reported that the headmaster of Winchester derived an income, from all sources, of £3,000 per annum (plus a rent-free house); the second master £1,500 per annum (plus free rooms in college). At Eton the headmaster's statutory emoluments were £375, his actual net income from all sources £4,500; the usher's stipend was about a quarter of the headmaster's (£78), but his actual net income was approximately three-quarters (£3,180).

The foundation statutes often distinguished meticulously between the state of the headmaster and his usher, prescribing inferior housing and other conditions of service for the latter. But in law the usher had a position virtually independent of the headmaster: he held his office by freehold tenure and was to all intents and purposes irremovable. He could be removed through action in the Court of Chancery, but this procedure was very expensive. The removal of a foundation master from Fremlington Endowed School cost £3,000 and impoverished the foundation.[32]

The usher often had complete control over the lower school and he recruited (and paid) his own assistant staff. The *London Evening Post* carried the following advertisement on 9 November 1731:

> Whereas Mr Franc. Goode, under-master at Eton, does hereby signify that there will be at Christmas next or soon after, two vacancies in his school, viz., as assistants to him and tutors to the young gents; if any two gentlemen of either university (who have commenced the degree of B.A. at least) shall think themselves duly qualified, and are desirous of such employment, let them enquire at Mr G's own house at Eaton College.

The usher was in fact a second headmaster and the endowed schools of England were paralysed by this dualism.

The usher's power derived principally from his ability to control the flow of pupils into the upper school. As the regulator of transfer arrangements, he could keep boys down and deprive the headmaster of pupils. The headmaster of Felsted once complained that the usher

> set up Altar against Altar and he thinks it hath given him an independent authority and that he hath a province of his own, where he supposes himself supream. He takes of himself admission without any knowledge of mine and where our founder ordered the Grammar he brings in the Horn-Book for his own ends. He also keeps the boys down ... for lucre's sake.[33]

The Clarendon and Taunton Commissions found such deadlock and paralysis widespread in the middle of the nineteenth century, and it was on their recommendation that the reorganized schools placed the usher in a position of due subordination. Another solution was to make the lower school a separate establishment and the usher the headmaster – a solution found at Harrow in the form of the Lower School of John Lyon and at Rugby in the School of

Lawrence Sherif. The Taunton Commission went to the heart of the matter by recommending the abolition of freehold tenure of office for all foundation masters:

> It is usually conceded that to pay the masters simply by handing over to them the whole or part of the proceeds of the endowment, and to give them a freehold tenure of their appointment, is a mere accident of the foundation, and that it ought not to be continued.[34]

The subjection of the usher and the supremacy of the headmaster date from the late Victorian period: both were contrived through the remodelling of public and endowed schools under the terms of the Public Schools Act of 1868 and the Endowed Schools Act of 1869. Control over internal organization was invested firmly and unambiguously in the headmaster; and

> the staffing of the schools was, in the great majority of cases, placed wholly in the hands of the headmasters. They were given full powers to appoint and dismiss their assistants and, provided that the total expenditure did not exceed a fixed sum, to pay them whatever salaries they considered advisable. The supremacy of the nineteenth-century headmaster in his school was thus based upon his possessing all the powers of the nineteenth-century employer.[35]

Thring at Uppingham and Sanderson at Oundle are only the better-known examples of powerful headmasters in the late nineteenth century. The historian of Oundle has said of Sanderson that staff 'must, in the main, see eye to eye with him; if they did not, they must go'.[36] Staff meetings under Thring were an ordeal: 'Those who had the task of disputing a question with him, had a task more stimulating than pleasant. They snatched a fearful joy in it . . . [for he] would disagree in accents which were felt to condemn.'[37]

Revised schemes of school government had placed late-Victorian headmasters in a powerful position. They often attempted detailed regulation of their schools, and were successful in their attempts. T. C. Fry, appointed headmaster of Oundle in 1883, required staff to remain on school premises when they were not teaching and issued detailed, written instructions on teaching methods. Pugnacious and autocratic, he threw himself into his task with such zeal that he burned himself out in a year. During this brief period he fought housemasters and Old Boys and showed a businesslike efficiency which impressed the Governors. Appointed at thirty-seven, he retired with a nervous breakdown when he was thirty-eight.[38]

The power of assistant masters increased only slowly. At least in the famous schools, men of high qualifications were recruited in the later nineteenth century and their quality made them a power to be taken seriously. The reformed universities were producing a much larger output of graduates of intellectual distinction. Many found careers in the restructured public and imperial service; but many more found their way into the schools. Between 1850 and 1880 the older universities, after remaining stationary in numbers for more than two centuries, doubled their numbers. In the thirty-seven years from 1850 to 1887 freshmen at Cambridge increased by 150 per cent.[39] The public schools and grammar schools of late-Victorian England were able to recruit from talented and able men.

James Wilson, headmaster of Clifton from 1879 to 1890, described his period of office as 'an age of great assistant masters'. Wilson was a practical administrator; he was not a great scholar, and his manner was didactic, but he ran a successful and efficient school. He was meticulous in his attention to detail. He attributed his success to his staff of exceptionally able men:

> I was astonished and uplifted at Clifton by the magnificent and helpful spirit of masters and boys. I cannot exaggerate this. It was a splendid staff of masters, some of whom were of quite exceptional ability. The school did what bees are said to do when they have accidentally lost their queen. They gather round an ordinary bee and make a queen of it.[40]

Henry Hayman at Rugby in the eighteen-seventies quite failed to appreciate the qualities and resourcefulness of his staff and within five years was driven from office. He was appointed in 1869 as Temple's successor. Temple judged him a self-willed and autocratic man 'who would never be able to work with the best type of assistant master'.[41] Even before he took up his appointment the assistant masters sent one of their number to demand that he withdraw from the headmastership. They had checked up on his testimonials and discovered that they were of doubtful reliability. (It is perhaps a sign of pre-bureaucratic appointment that personal recommendation, as distinct from formal qualifications, was still so very important. When Henry Montagu Butler applied – unsuccessfully – for Harrow in 1859 he supplied thirty-one testimonials from bishops and men of similar eminence; when Jex-Blake applied for Haileybury in 1867 he supplied sixty-five testimonials which were printed and bound in book form.)

Hayman took up his appointment and was immediately at loggerheads with his staff over elections to the new governing body and appointments to boarding houses. He ignored established custom in the matter of promotions and engaged in bitter conflict with the staff. He refused to assign pupils to A. E. Scott, whom he locked out of his classroom. Scott, with the help of the boys, took desks through the window and held his class in the Close. The final victory went to the assistant masters: after five embattled years, the Governors dismissed Hayman in 1874.

Neither headmasters nor their assistants were, in general, well paid in the late nineteenth century. The Taunton Commission observed in 1868 that 'The general remuneration both of head and assistant masters is low, excepting where a large boarding house is kept.'[42] But the gap between headmasters and their assistants was a good deal wider than today. Some notion of the differential considered appropriate may be gained from the recommendation of the Clarendon Commission in 1864 that the headmaster of Winchester should receive £2,500 per annum, assistant masters on average one-fifth of this – a range from £200 to £800 per annum. In 1895 the average income of assistant masters in grammar schools was £135 per annum;[43] but three-quarters of headmasters had salaries in excess of £200 per annum.[44] Salaries of assistant masters at Eton, Harrow and Rugby were high (rising from £600 to £1,600 at Rugby), but in general £150 was considered a good salary for an assistant master. The majority of headmasters earned twice as much,[45] within a range from £200 to £500; a dozen or so had incomes between £500 and £2,000.[46] This contrasts strongly with the situation in 1970 when a good honours graduate assistant master in his forties earns approximately two-thirds of the salary of a good honours headmaster of the same age – some £2,000 compared with the latter's £3,000.[47]

Assistants were not only ill-paid in late-Victorian England; they were extremely insecure. At Rugby under Arnold high salaries were some compensation for insecurity: 'The staff saved a good deal of their salary, as indeed they had to, for permanent entrenchment at Rugby was not encouraged.'[48] Headmasters were not only much better paid, they were much more secure. In the first half of the nineteenth century 78 per cent of the assistant masters at Shrewsbury left after less than ten years, 58 per cent left after less than five years; but two headmasters, Butler and Kennedy, covered the entire period 1800 to 1859. A few eminent schools afforded greater security, but 'outside this very small circle the situation was deplorable, with very poor pay, a life of subservience and, for the realist, very little to look forward to.'[49]

There was no incremental salary scale for teachers, and few superannuation schemes. A change of headmaster often meant the dismissal of the entire staff. In 1899 the retiring headmaster of Grantham School dismissed his three assistant masters; the new head told them a few days before the new term began that he would not re-engage them because he had brought his own men. Evidence of such practices was given to the Royal Commission on Secondary Education in 1895: 'when you dismiss the headmaster you dismiss every man in his school'.[50] The Assistant Masters' Association, founded in 1891, first campaigned for assistants to be no longer the employees of the headmaster, but of the governing bodies. This was finally achieved in the Endowed Schools (Masters) Act of 1908.

Schools have become more bureaucratized over the past century in the sense that they have become more hierarchical. The Burnham Committee, especially since the Second World War, has defined status levels for salary purposes, distinguishing between departmental heads of varying importance, and other assistant masters with 'graded posts' and appropriate allowances. The power to recommend his staff for these more highly remunerated posts has given the headmaster an important form of patronage. While assistant masters have quite remarkable powers inside their classrooms, headmasters still have remarkable powers outside. They can still assign assistant masters to teach the classes and even the subjects that they think fit. They have scarcely questioned powers in the matter of job allocation.

But bureaucratization has meant more power for all. Modern bureaucracies do not necessarily reduce a man's sense of power or induce 'alienation'. On the contrary, they probably, in general, promote a sense of power and reduce alienation. There is probably a curvilinear relationship between members' sense of power, satisfaction and attachment, and the degree of bureaucratization. When organizations have muted bureaucratic features – few rules, infrequent checking up by superiors, and de-emphasized status differences – members at all levels of the organization may feel insecure, uncertain, and even neglected. Research by the author into the attitudes and satisfactions of sandwich course students working in industry indicates that this may be the case. The bureaucracies in which they worked were scaled according to hierarchy of authority, participation in decision-making, job codifications, and rule observation.[51] The subjects' satisfactions declined with bureaucratic severity. Nevertheless, very infrequent supervision, like very frequent supervision, was associated with unfavourable attitudes.[52]

There is stronger evidence of the supportive nature of bureaucratic organization in American research into teachers' attitudes and satisfactions. One inquiry carried out in twenty schools of varying size and organization set out to test the notion that teachers in highly bureaucratized schools would have a much lower sense of power than teachers in less bureaucratic systems. Schools were rated by people who knew them well on a range of bureaucratic attributes like the hierarchy of authority, the system of rules, the division of labour, and the impersonality of interaction. The teachers indicated their sense of power by responding to questions about their involvement in decisions affecting various areas of school life and work. The unequivocal result was that teachers in highly bureaucratic schools had a significantly greater sense of power. This held true when a range of significant variables were controlled, such as the social origin of teachers, their length of service in the school, and the extent of their contact with school officials.[53]

We have had a tragic view of bureaucracy in recent times,

especially perhaps, since William H. Whyte published *The Organization Man* in 1956. This view does not stand up when comparisons are made between modern bureaucratic employment and comparable pre-bureaucratic employment; or when modern bureaucratic employment is compared with earlier forms of bureaucratic employment. The large and rule-regulated comprehensive school offers a qualified teacher incomparably greater power and dignity than was possible even for a Fellow of the Royal Society – and there were many such – who worked as a private tutor in an eighteenth-century household. It is true that we have no foolproof bureaucratic device which will entirely neutralize the top man who is a bully; but teachers are no longer a servile race; bureaucracy has been their salvation.

8 The good headteacher

The good leader is aloof and gives praise sparingly. He hoards approval, keeps it scarce, and so maintains its value. He communicates infrequently with his subordinates and, if he is a school headmaster, he is unlikely to have taken courses in educational administration. His staff see his authority as legitimate not only by virtue of his appointment according to established procedures, but because he has appropriate academic qualifications and relevant experience of suitable duration. He has suffered as they have. He 'interferes' in the work of his assistant staff, but he protects them from outside interference. He is often off the premises. He innovates unceasingly. He sets difficult goals, which are constantly revised, and insists on their attainment. He accepts the hatred of his subordinates as inevitable and selects as his deputy a man who is at least as skilled in diplomacy, and schooled in tact and discretion, as he is ingenious in constructing timetables. If he prides himself on running 'one big, happy family', he is probably a disaster.

The headmaster is in difficulty from the outset because the qualities which gained him promotion have little bearing on his new tasks. He has been effective with his pupils as a classteacher and perhaps more generally (at least in grammar and public schools) as a 'schoolmaster'; now he must be effective as an organizer and co-ordinator of other people's front-line activities. Until the later nineteenth century there was no such marked discontinuity between the job of an assistant master and a head. The headmaster remained essentially a teacher but, on promotion, he concentrated his attention on the older boys, especially in the Sixth. His job was to inspire the Sixth and set an example to his assistant staff who taught the younger boys.

The new headmaster might have been promoted because he had become famous for a new teaching 'system', and his job was to commend this system to his staff. But often he had little authority to impose it; he could only hope that it might be contagious. Samuel Butler at Shrewsbury between 1798 and 1836 is a good illustration of the great teacher-headmaster. He also illustrates the impotence of the pre-bureaucratic head over matters of educational procedure. Butler tried for thirty-seven years to control the teaching methods and disciplinary arrangements throughout his school and entirely failed to do so. Jendwine, the Second Master, regarded Butler's recommendations as 'interference' and continued in his own way.[1] The nineteenth-century headmaster was often in difficulty because he was principally a super-teacher; the modern headmaster is in difficulty because he is not.

Yet often he has earned promotion through his reputation as a super-teacher, and even because he is famous for a 'system'. He may have written books and addressed professional conferences. Since the Second World War he will probably have gained a reputation as a 'progressive' and an innovator. There has been a postwar imperative for aspiring teachers not to uphold traditions but to subvert them. This means, in brief, that the new head will have opposed streaming, corporal punishment, eleven-plus selection, single-sex education, insulation from parents, the prefect system (unless elective), traditional examinations, didactic or even expository class teaching – and, above all, he will have paid special attention to 'group work'. In recent years he will have espoused the teacher-group as well as the pupil-group: he will have been a champion of team-teaching. And he will talk approvingly and even knowledgeably about educational technology.

As a headmaster he has ceased to be an unattached (and irresponsible) intellectual. He has become a bureaucrat. And he suffers the common fate of intellectuals in bureaucracies: he is under pressure 'to temper the wind to the shorn lamb, that is, to fit his original abstract formulations to the exigencies of the situation.'[2] If he makes this adjustment he will be seen by many as 'selling out';

if he does not, he may find that he is virtually obliged to look for a lectureship in a college of education.

The new headmaster may find that he must modify his most cherished theories; more seriously, he may find that he has no time to indulge in theories at all. His activities as an educational theorist, or as a scholar in his own academic discipline, may be submerged beneath the day-to-day bureaucratic obligations of the job. In an American study of school principals, a majority felt they spent too much time on 'managing the school office'; they found burdensome such tasks as taking inventories of equipment and preparing reports for higher authorities.[3] Taylor's study of principals in English training colleges similarly showed how widely 'administrative trivia' were resented. Principals wanted more time for teaching, research, writing and personal study, more respite from their instrumental and manipulative tasks. Taylor observes:

> Principals are, in fact, the best academically qualified group in the training colleges.... But the principal's task is not conducive to the maintenance of a high level of academic effort....
>
> In sum, the present situation involves a progressive bureaucratization of the principal's role, and a limitation of his opportunities to provide academic leadership within the college.[4]

A nineteenth-century headmaster could run his school and make a serious contribution to scholarship. It was, indeed, an expectation that he should do both. Senior positions in schools, like senior positions in the civil service, did not preclude scholarly or literary pursuits. Anthony Trollope in the Post Office, James Mill at the India Office, Matthew Arnold in Her Majesty's Inspectorate and his father in the headmastership at Rugby combined scholarship with the conduct of responsible administrative offices. The higher levels of the civil service counted distinguished and active scholars like Sir James Headlam-Morley, the historian, and Sir Arthur Hirtzel, the Virgilian scholar, among its most accomplished members. The civil servant J. N. MacKail was awarded the O.M., not for his acknowledged distinction in administration, but for his contribution to letters. A. J. Toynbee has maintained that such men were better bureaucrats precisely because their wider intellectual life gave them 'a better chance of retaining – or developing – a sense of proportion'.[5] A sense of proportion is ever less likely. The scope of the operations of the civil service in the twentieth century has made these wider activities impossible for its members. The same is true of schools. It is unthinkable today that a public school headmaster might do work which led to the offer of an Oxford professorship – as happened to Arnold while he was headmaster of Rugby. The welfare functions of schools in particular have probably made the headmaster's administrative work increasingly burdensome. He no longer has time for the academic interests which led to his promotion. In fact power is distinctly dull, its exercise felt to be a tedious burden. The source of power for headmasters is their bureaucratic office rather than their personal charisma. The problems of recruiting able men to boring positions of power in schools as in other organizations may in the future be a serious one.

The headmaster's office gives him authority; his staff accord him commensurate power only if he exhibits appropriate characteristics. 'Two prerequisites of leadership are a position of dominance and the legitimating approval of followers....'[6] Succession is an occasion for scrutinizing the legitimacy of the successor, his qualifications for office, and the way he obtained it. Legitimating characteristics of headteachers are probably defined differently by different categories of teacher. Assistant staff expect the head to have had 'relevant' teaching experience of suitable duration, and to have good academic qualifications, especially if he is the head of a grammar school. His professional (as distinct from his academic) qualifications may have impressed the appointing committee; they are unlikely to impress his subordinates. The higher degree of Master of Education, no less than the postgraduate certificate in education, is likely to be treated as at best an irrelevance. His appointment will be legitimated in the eyes of his staff above all by his teaching experience: they will judge less than six or seven years as too little, more than fifteen or sixteen as too much. And he will be judged after his appointment for his expertness in co-ordinating activity and taking a firm line with pupils, parents and the education authority. His staff will support him not if he claims the right to coerce or even to reward, but if he shows that he has 'expert-power'.[7] Today the proper expertise is likely to be seen as bureaucratic rather than pedagogic.[8]

Appointing committees may consider 'relevant experience' a serious disqualification because it produces 'narrowness', and, in consequence, they may appoint 'irregulars'. H.M.I.s have commonly been irregulars, appointed not because they had teaching experience in the kind of school they would inspect, but because they had not. The famous Holmes-Morant circular of 1910, like the report of the Newcastle Commission (on elementary education) of 1861, regarded elementary teachers as creatures of routine, unfitted by their experience for appointment to H.M. Inspectorate:

> As compared with the ex-elementary teacher usually engaged in the hopeless task of surveying or trying to survey a wide field of education from a well-worn groove, the Inspector of public schools of the 'varsity type has the advantage of being able to look at elementary education from a point of view of complete detachment, and therefore of being able to handle its problems with freshness and originality.[9]

Irrelevant experience appears to have been an important qualification for appointment to secondary modern school headships in the nineteen-fifties, and likewise to principalships of colleges of education. Suitable academic and social talents were imported from other spheres. A survey of 131 college of education principals conducted in the early nineteen-sixties showed that 'forty per cent of the men and nearly twenty per cent of the women had never worked in a training college prior to becoming principals'.[10] Universities commonly select men with experience of university teaching and administration as their vice-chancellors, although 'those coming from the civil service or the diplomatic corps are a small but growing minority'.[11] Experience in little-related fields of life may ensure 'detachment', even 'freshness and originality'; but it may put the headmaster, principal or vice-chancellor at a serious disadvantage with subordinates, who expect him to have a detailed and first-hand knowledge of their problems. And as a non-combatant his promotion smacks of immorality (and if he has been a combatant, of desertion). His discomfiture and inexperience may enable his subordinates to consolidate their power.

In any case he is likely to have trouble with the 'Rebecca Myth',[12] especially if he is succeeding a charismatic headmaster famous as a successful innovator and pioneer. The charismatic innovator succeeding a traditionalist is in no less trouble. Assistant masters who resented the erstwhile autocratic rule will now observe that at least decent order was maintained, exercises were marked (and marked on an intelligible scale), lessons began on time, and boys sent to be flogged would assuredly be flogged.

The problems inherent in succession will be faced by the new headmaster according to his conception of promotion: he may see it primarily as reward for past achievements (including the gaining of formal qualifications); or he may see it primarily as compensation for all the troubles ahead. Teachers may be more prone than salesmen or industrial managers to see promotion as reward rather than compensation, an honour like a knighthood or a D.S.O. which looks to the past rather than the future. Promotion both recognizes talent and puts it to further test. In practice, it is asymmetrical, the greater the past achievement the easier the future task. The well-qualified man with a very successful record can – and often does – command the more attractive, less demanding post. The least accomplished have to take on the more difficult jobs. When a well-established grammar school in a good residential suburb needs a new headmaster, there is no dearth of well-qualified applicants who clearly have not come forward as missionaries.

If he bases his legitimacy mainly on his past achievements – even a housemastership, a military decoration and a Ph.D. – rather than proposals for the future, the new headmaster is likely to meet resistance from his staff. The effective leader is innovatory, forward-looking: his staff never know what to expect next. The effective headmaster will constantly promote change though its educational purpose is obscure or even non-existent. There is no plateau on which he can safely rest. Headteachers see themselves (probably correctly) as more innovatory and educationally progressive than their assistants (and there appears to be no tendency for their innovatory zeal to decline with age).[13] They pay a price in staff resentment; but the returns are high.

Innovation promotes uncertainty and enlarges a manager's area of discretion. If his authority is closely defined and procedures are regulated in detail, he has little scope for the exercise of power; in such circumstances he has a special interest in innovation. Crozier has described the urge for innovation among conservative managers in a closely regulated French bureaucracy: change, against all their finer instincts, is their only strategy of power.

> The directors' strategy, therefore, is to fight for change.... Whatever their own feelings at the beginning, they adopt the strategy of technological change. They come to understand that the only possible way to increase their own power and put the technical engineers back in their subordinate place is to impose large-scale changes within the plant. They are in favour of technical progress not for ideological reasons, but for strategic ones.[14]

Innovation generates power, puts more into the system. Directors of Education who pioneered the reorganization (or comprehensivization) of secondary education gained power from doing so. They may already have been more powerful in order to introduce their schemes ahead of their time, as in the Leicestershire Plan of the 'fifties; they were made still more powerful than most by carrying them through. Their enhanced power was mainly at the expense of headmasters, especially in the grammar schools; but as headmasters themselves joined the innovatory movement, their power was increased, in turn, *vis-à-vis* their assistant staff. Power thrives on uncertainty. Powerful headmasters and education officers will already be planning the reorganization of the reorganized schools.

The good headmaster will remain aloof from his assistant staff but he will interfere with their work. His 'task-orientation' (concern with getting difficult jobs successfully completed) will make him unpopular and lonely; in these circumstances lies his power.

The famous Hawthorne studies at the Western Electric Company's Chicago works, carried out between 1927 and 1932, appeared to support 'democratic' leadership, open and abundant communication, and participation by all ranks in decision-making. Social factors at work, such as warm, informal and non-punitive supervision, appeared to be more important for productivity than economic rewards. 'None of the results (of the Hawthorne investigations) gave the slightest substantiation to the theory that the worker is primarily motivated by economic interest', it was alleged.[15] The classical economists' 'economic man' was apparently a myth. Happiness in human relationships at work seemed to be of paramount importance.

These influential studies of Elton Mayo and his associates have had far-reaching consequences for the practice of education, as they have for the conduct of industry. Their consequences for the behaviour of teachers are discussed elsewhere in this book. Here some of the implications for the headmaster's relationship with his staff will be considered.

A headmaster has recently recalled, with obvious approval and even relish, his own schooldays in a pre-Mayo era, under a headmaster whose regime

> was ferociously personal. He had a telephone for external communication, which he kept to a minimum, and a cane, which he used less sparingly, for internal rule.... We passed our Matric and won university scholarships because we dared not deprive him of his Speech Day records and percentages.

Hard work came from determined goal-setting and extrinsic rewards. Whereas the earlier headmaster came in to morning assembly like Jehovah, his former pupil assumes a more muted headmasterly style: he 'sidles on to the platform hoping to remain as unnoticed as possible'.[16] Overly 'dominative' leadership styles have become as discreditable in schools as in factories.

The original Hawthorne studies have themselves been intensively studied; and their large claims have been found to lack adequate support.[17] One critical re-examination of the evidence has focused on the five girls who were taken from the factory floor and placed in a special, experimental work-room.[18] Much of the evidence relating to supervisory styles derives from the behaviour and performance of these girls, whose productivity increased by 30 per cent over a two-year period.

Their improved performance was attributed by the researchers to changes in non-material circumstances, notably to very light constraints and friendly relationships with supervisors. A close examination of the records shows that in any case the girls were unusual; they had been specially selected because they were known to be willing, co-operative and competent. Even so, under the less exacting control of the experimental room, they talked so much among themselves that eventually two were dismissed for 'gross insubordination'. The two replacements had heavy family responsibilities and every reason to work hard and encourage their co-workers to do so.

After careful scrutiny of the available evidence the following conclusions emerge:

> there would seem to be good grounds for supposing that supervision became more friendly and relaxed because output increased rather than vice versa.

> The results of these studies, far from supporting the various components of the 'human relations approach', are surprisingly consistent with a rather old-fashioned view about the value of monetary incentives, driving leadership, and discipline.

Recent studies of English factory workers cast doubt on the importance for morale and productivity of warm relationships at work in general, and of warm relationships with the supervisor in particular. The car factory assembly-line workers appeared to attach little importance to close and stable relationships with their fellows; they did not seem to be in need of 'expressive leadership' from the foreman. There was little antagonism towards foremen; but neither was there particular affection. The workers approved of the foreman who communicates infrequently: 'he leaves you alone, you scarcely ever see him'.[19]

The supervision of semi-skilled factory workers is not the same thing as the leadership of professional employees, such as teachers, who have a claim to a considerable measure of autonomy. But one (American) study of staff leadership in schools points to the importance of making exacting demands and insisting that they be met. Gross and Herriott were interested in the special case of superiors dealing with subordinates who are judged capable of performing their tasks 'in an essentially autonomous manner'.[20]

Their study, which was carried out in 175 schools, was concerned with leadership conceived as the 'obligation to improve the quality of staff performance'. More than thirteen hundred teachers rated their principals on an 'executive professional leadership' scale. Scale items referred to aiding, advising and encouraging teachers in their work. Scale scores were related to organizational features of the schools and to the personal characteristics of the principals.

There was no tendency for principals who had taken advanced courses in educational studies in general, or educational administration in particular, to obtain high leadership scores; there was a tendency for the score to decline with age. (A good record in academic, as distinct from professional, studies did, however, correlate positively with the E.P.L. scores.) But the central findings of this study seem to be two: firstly, principals highly rated as leaders had staff who were judged highly efficient and whose pupils learned a lot; secondly, there were clear indications that the exercise of professional leadership by principals was disliked by their staff. A complementary inquiry into teachers' and principals' conceptions of the amount of control the principal should exercise gave 'support for the assumption of teacher resistance to the principal's professional leadership'.[21]

In short, the teachers regarded the effective leader as an 'interfering' leader. He was positive and forceful; but he improved the professional performance of his staff. The authors of this study are in no doubt that leaders should lead; all cannot safely be left to a sense of professional responsibility or the self-regulating interaction of a group of equals. 'The findings, in short, offer empirical support for a leadership conception of the principal's role, and they undermine a major argument for abandoning it.'[22]

A more traditional view of effective leadership is being reinstated by a number of studies that have been made in recent years to test the claims and assumptions of the 'human relations school'. Often they confirm ancient wisdom, for example on the disadvantages of close personal involvement with subordinates. Emotional nepotism, like actual nepotism, has for long been observed by men of sense to make for less efficient working of organizations. Controlled observation and experimentation by social scientists points to a similar conclusion.

High status is a tool for doing difficult jobs; low status is a protection from inappropriate demands by superiors. If power in education is to be expanded, there is a case for augmenting status conferred by the job from outside sources: there should be knighthoods and peerages for assistant masters and for headmasters. Requests to parents, Old Boys, directors of education, universities and even pupils are likely to be more carefully attended to if one is a baron as well as the senior history master. And the protection of low status should not be undermined through personal friendship with superiors: requests which exceed the normal expectations of the post should not be made 'as a personal favour'. Status barriers are important protective devices for the young and inexperienced.

Fiedler has investigated the effect of a leader's 'social distance' from his followers. His method of measuring social distance was curiously indirect, based on leaders' ratings of themselves and their associates on various attributes. Leaders who rate their most and least preferred co-workers quite differently are assumed to be willing to recognize subordinates' deficiencies: they do not suffer fools gladly. They are prepared to reject any person who is a poor co-worker, irrespective of other, personal considerations. Leaders of basketball teams, surveying parties and sales co-operatives had more successful teams if they were 'socially distant' from their followers in these terms. These aloof leaders were presumed to be effective because they had less difficulty in implementing difficult and perhaps distasteful but necessary decisions.[23]

As he grows further from subordinates in age, a leader may feel that he runs less risk in getting closer to them in personal relationships. Recent research into headteachers' conceptions of their role indicates that headteachers over fifty years of age are far more inclined than younger heads to favour involvement in the personal problems of pupils, staff and parents. They are more inclined to agree that a head should meet members of staff informally in his own home and know them well enough to help them with personal problems in connection with their work as teachers.[24] A wider age-gap probably makes possible a reduction in social distance.

Later studies by Fiedler led to some refinement and qualification of his original argument, but appeared to support it in essence. These later studies led to the conclusion that a leader's aloofness would be effective in task, as opposed to social, groups; and that it would be ineffective if the leader was not trusted by his own superiors.

The good headteacher 117

But within these limits, a leader's social distance would tend to lead to more efficient performance by his followers. He would lead effectively not only because he was free to discipline followers, with whom he had no emotional involvement, but also because his aloof demeanor made his subordinates uncertain and anxious.[25]

Anxiety, tension and unhappiness are seen by Argyris as essential attributes of successful superior–subordinate relationships. The successful executive in industry promoted anxiety in the supervisors under him by putting them under pressure: he checked on their performance, set goals for them which he constantly revised, and dealt separately with them as a means of dividing and controlling them. Tension is seen by Argyris as an essential motivating force leading to learning and creativity: '... if people are not led to be at all dissatisfied with their current performance and experience no anxiety whatsoever, the learning process may not proceed at all.'[26]

The good leader is aloof and gives approval sparingly. Studies of naval cadets at Duke University have suggested that unstinted approval of others is incompatible with superior status. It is, as common sense and observation indicate, people of inferior status who give approval freely.[27] Other studies have pointed to this conclusion: that effective informal leaders are more sparing and discriminating in their approval of their followers than are ineffective leaders.[28] Praise and encouragement are husbanded and their value enhanced.

A leader by definition controls and constrains; his followers incur the 'cost' of not doing what they might otherwise have done. If he leads them to valued goals their hatred may diminish, but perhaps, as Homans maintains, the best he can hope for 'is that the things he is liked for should increase a little faster than the things he is disliked for.'[29] In schools the attainment of valued goals is less obvious, immediate and dramatic than in many enterprises, and the headmaster's reward for constraining his staff correspondingly reduced. A team of engineers building a bridge, of surgeons performing a difficult operation, of soldiers attacking an enemy position, may achieve spectacular and undisputed success. Open scholarships and G.C.E. examination results are a headmaster's most tangible evidence that the discipline he imposes pays off; and he is likely to cherish these accordingly. If his team does not compete for such prizes, his inevitable unpopularity may remain undiminished. Close and familiar social intercourse with his staff will be no solution. As Homans has argued: 'authority over a man and social equality with him are, in our terms, incongruent'. 'If indeed he [the leader] persists in acting familiarly he will cast doubt on his superiority in power.'[30]

The good headmaster will make of loneliness an effective tool of command; but if he is necessarily socially distant, this is precisely why his deputy must not be. The abrasions which have properly and necessarily been caused by the headmaster must be soothed by his deputy, if the team is to co-operate effectively. The headmaster and his deputy constitute a 'leadership-alliance'. They are complementary in their function, the former providing instrumental or task-oriented leadership, the latter expressive or social-emotional leadership.[31] Headmasters, like principals of colleges of education,[32] may be fretful at their primarily instrumental role and hanker for the opportunity to engage in relaxed, expressive relationships with their staff. But if the headmaster insists on being friends, his deputy may have to be their enemy. The head who makes frequent ritual visits to the staffroom for coffee at morning break, to show that he is a friendly fellow, affable and accessible, may put everyone under unnecessary and unproductive strain, especially his deputy. Friendship is the deputy's job. Headmasters often expect their deputies to bear the brunt of rule enforcement while they themselves specialize in good relations with staff, pupils, parents and public. It is true that a headmaster's role is largely a diplomatic role, but it is external relationships that are his special concern. He is the link with the wider world, and will usually insist that all communications from outside come through him, that all visitors to the school, for whatever purpose, should meet him on entry and departure. Headmasters are filters of the external world. Principals of colleges of education commonly have similar expectations with respect to visitors, and in this they differ markedly from university vice-chancellors. This is not necessarily because the latter are busier men or control larger institutions. A headmaster's control over all external communications is a good indicator of the remarkable power position that he still enjoys.

The good headmaster is frequently away from school and is

consequently reviled in the staffroom for not doing his job. But it is by getting into the outside world that he does it. He is sensitive to parental views and generally wishes to take them into account but, as Cohen has shown, he believes that his staff oppose his openness to such outside influences. Cohen's research on a national sample of headteachers shows that they think that teachers in general are unconvinced of the wisdom of close parent–teacher co-operation and wish contact with parents to be infrequent, formal and ritualized. Headmasters are in general convinced of the need for a close liaison with parents.[33]

The deputy headmaster specializes in internal communication. In particular he is the link between the headmaster and the assistant staff: 'he is classically poised between the head's study and the classroom'.[34] He is a communications expert, although the head may see him as primarily concerned with routine organization – timetables, room allocation and examination schedules. A study of 277 deputy heads in secondary modern and grammar schools showed that they conceive their duties differently. They see their job as requiring first and foremost skills in dealing with the school staff, listening to their problems, suggesting solutions, and interceding with the head on their behalf. They do not see themselves primarily as organizers; they consider that 'concern for teachers' is the most important part of their job. When asked what advice they would give an aspiring deputy head they were agreed that he should develop his skills in dealing with people. Their main complaint was that the head delegates responsibilities, but does not delegate sufficient power to discharge them.[35]

One of the rewards of high status is the deference of others. This may be why people in senior positions are often much involved in social life. Their sociability is a consequence and not a cause of their promotion to high office. But the indications are that they should be sociable with other people's subordinates, and not with those for whom they have direct responsibility. The headmaster will find the gratifications of office at the golf clubs and the Rotarians. On the school premises he must accept loneliness and learn to turn it to good account.

9 The power environment

Schools and colleges have various linkages with society, by which they are circumscribed and constrained. They exist in power environments. There are various strategies of adaptation to the pressures of the power environment, varying from capitulation through coalition, co-optation and bargaining, to outright revolt;[1] but in varying degrees all schools are constrained by their power environments and limited in their ability to choose and to attain their goals. Primary schools and technical colleges appear to be at opposite poles of environmental constraint. The linkages which will receive special attention in this chapter will be two: the human 'input' and 'output'. Schools are crucially linked to the wider society by what goes into them and what comes out – by the characteristics of their product. In particular, power relations in schools are likely to be influenced by the extent to which they produce a standardized output for social consumption, as distinct from more variable, custom-built models. One reason why the contemporary school is at the same time authoritarian and underpowered is that its output is standardized and predictable.

The power environment of a school or college may include some or all of the following: central government departments, the local education authority, examining bodies, employers, professional associations, teachers' associations and subject associations. Parents vary in the pressures they exert according to their social class position and their children's age.[2] Some pressure groups may be handled through formal machinery of incorporation, in parent–teacher associations, governing bodies, and the Council or Convocation of universities. Old Boys and alumni have often been important elements in the power environment, both informally – as in the bitter power struggles which occurred at Rugby and other public schools in the mid-nineteenth century; and formally, as provided for in the machinery of government especially in the Universities of Oxford, Cambridge and London. Today Old Boys and alumni seem to be principally important as fund-raisers; but as late as 1909 Lord Curzon could ask, when a university Convocation appeared to be threatened: 'Would it not be handing over the university to an oligarchy of resident teachers, to some extent detached from the outside world, and independent of its criticism?'[3]

The importance of the social environment to the functioning of formal organizations has been de-emphasized by social scientists over the past three or four decades. Those who followed Elton Mayo in a 'human relations' approach to behaviour in factories, offices and schools, saw the organization suspended in a social vacuum: effort, morale, productivity, labour-turnover, and the authority structure were explained in terms of internal circumstances, notably by involvement in informal groups. This was the broad conclusion of the celebrated 'Hawthorne studies'; and Mayo interpreted his war-time investigations of industrial productivity along similar lines. In accounting for behaviour at work, external relationships and attachments were irrelevant:

> the characteristic divisions of our former society account for little or nothing. Among individual members [of work-groups] are included coloured people, some Californians, men and women of Oklahoma and Arkansas (and there's ordinarily great difficulty of association for Californians with 'Okies' and 'Arkies'), and many others. We have indeed been surprised throughout this country during the war – East, Mid-West, and California – by the ease with which coloured people, and others, are absorbed into a working group if and when they have clearly 'made the team'.[4]

On the basis of such inquiries and observations Mayo erected a theory not only of insulated work-groups, but of self-regulating social units. Men were not by nature a rabble requiring external control. The formal constraints of authority were in any case as ineffectual as external affiliations. Mayo's neo-anarchism was located in a social void.[5]

Critics of Mayo who have re-emphasized the formal structure of organizations have also paid scant attention to their social context: their studies have been essentially comparative, seeking a general theory of organizations which will embrace factories, schools, armies, hospitals and all formal systems whatever their origins and purposes.[6] But Crozier's recent studies of French bureaucracies have shown how the examination of formal organization and of the social context are interdependent: the authority structures of government departments arise not only from strictly organizational needs, but also from the French cultural system as a whole, with its hostility to submission to face-to-face authority relationships. Organizational rules are needed not only to get jobs done, but to implement important cultural values by protecting workers at different levels from each other. Organizational needs appear, indeed, to be largely thwarted by the influence of the wider culture.[7]

Schools vary in their openness to the external social environment. Public schools and primary schools, for different reasons, and in different ways, appear to be near the closed end of the spectrum; technical colleges are at the open end. Traditional grammar schools are in an intermediate, partially closed position.

Wakeford has emphasized the discontinuity between the public (boarding) school and the wider society. The public school is, by its nature, 'a highly distinctive and specific kind of organization. The way of life within it does not in any direct way "represent" life outside it. Many of the roles, values and activities have no direct counterparts outside the school organization.'[8] Indeed, the public school is in many respects a counter-society, deliberately insulating itself from the wider world, maximizing its autonomy. It stands at the opposite pole to the technical colleges and the technological universities, which deliberately contrive the maximum of interpenetration with the industrial environment through their sandwich course arrangements (as well as the representation of industrial interests in their governing bodies).

There is no doubt that the sandwich course generally fails to achieve the 'integration' of academic study and industrial practice that its champions claim for it;[9] but it represents none the less a serious threat to the integrity and autonomy of colleges. This threat operates in two ways. First, through the promotion of industrial values within a university context, which stress the subservience of science to industrial-organizational goals rather than to the institutional goals of science.[10] Where such values prevail, even very senior academic men will find that it is 'natural' to be confined, restricted and directed in their choice of research problems and curricular arrangements. Secondly, the threat operates more crudely and directly through industry's supplying 'sponsored' sandwich course students.

These environmental restrictions in colleges of technology have been shrewdly commented on by well-qualified observers such as Jahoda and Trow. The former has discussed the issue as a boundary problem, and the danger as one of including industry, with its special and distinctive purposes, within the boundary of an educational system which has its own proper and distinctive objectives. The former Diploma of Technology which was offered by Brunel and the other colleges of advanced technology, could be regarded as an educational system with open boundaries to the industrial world; or it could be seen as including industry within its boundaries. In Jahoda's Brunel study,

> views of industrial personnel have emerged which clearly favour this second way of thinking about the diploma. The fact that industry pays works-based students during the college periods and all students during the training periods – a fact which understandably though wrongly creates the impression that industry pays wholly for this education – further supports this approach.[11]

Jahoda points out the dangers of this vulnerability to the industrial environment:

> The overwhelming counter-argument is that educational systems, in order to function with optimal efficiency, require an internal organization and order to establish priorities relevant to their central task. Now the central task of industry is obviously not the same as that of a college; if industry were regarded as within the educational system it would bring to it its own task

which would make chaos out of the situation; to establish priorities among the very different major concerns of each partner could be achieved only by sacrificing some aspect of one of the central tasks. At the various points at which the Diploma in Technology education has experienced difficulties, the reason lies more often than not in confusing the openness of the system with a state where the loose boundary embraces both systems.[12]

This is a circumspect and guarded description of a subservient educational system (as befits an author actually in the employ of a technological university); Martin Trow's strictures are more forthright (as befit a non-subservient, marauding American). He questions the wisdom, in any case, of training young men for industry rather than, in some sense, against it; and cogently argues the case for producing engineers whose values and orientation will make them abrasive to industrial management. He points to the deep-rooted incompatibility of industrial and academic values, and the impossibility of a university fulfilling its proper educative role if its values are co-extensive with those of industry. Only technicians can be produced where industrial values dominate, with education closely linked to the industrial environment. 'And the linkages are most evident in the sandwich course, which makes industrial experience part and parcel of the higher technical training.'

For the tone and climate of institutions which aim to produce technicians, of whatever degree of skill, is basically different from that which produces men who are to reform or modify current practice. Staff training, recruitment and basic orientations toward industry are different; their relations with the broader scientific and intellectual community are different; facilities and opportunities for research (i.e., for systematic scepticism regarding current practice) are different. To teach professional engineers and technicians in the same institutions, with the same staff and in a similar relationship to the community on the one hand and to science on the other, is to risk training engineers who are only a more knowledgeable variety of technician.[13]

The English primary school, according to Blyth, is remarkable for its independence of both its power and cultural environments.

(Conceivably its high level of autonomy is related to the adventurous curricular innovation and inventiveness for which it has been noted in recent decades. But public schools have not used their autonomy in a similar way, perhaps because they experience one major environmental constraint from which primary schools are free – their product enters directly into society.) Blyth's somewhat mystical and idealized account of the primary school ascribes its autonomy to a variety of social and psychological circumstances: to the nature of children in the so-called 'Midlands years', and the fact that for them, apparently, life is essentially 'school-centred';[14] and to the expectations of parents, pupils and teachers that the primary school ought to develop an autonomous role 'by cutting purposefully adrift from the culture-patterns associated with the various parts of its clientele and creating something new and worthwhile in itself.'[15] Perhaps more to the point is the progressive abolition of the eleven-plus examination which has freed primary schools from the constraints of external examinations – constraints which have increasingly restricted the freedom of action of schools at the secondary stage (even when they have opted for the more liberal modes of examining possible with the C.S.E., which have actually taken more decisions – about teaching methods as well as syllabuses – outside the schools[16]).

The sandwich course and external examinations are examples of an oppressive power environment; but they are exceptions to the general trend over the past century for the power environments of schools, colleges and universities to become less oppressive and restrictive. The trend was slowed down, but not reversed, by the failure, contrary to the recommendations of the Robbins Report (1963), to place the colleges of education in the autonomous sector of higher education; and by the refusal, in Mr Crosland's Woolwich speech (1966), to do likewise for the new polytechnics. While neither institution has achieved the autonomy accorded to the former colleges of advanced technology, both have moved far along the road of internal self-government. The recommendations of the Donnison Report (1970) would greatly accelerate the trend to moderate the impact of the power environment on secondary schools.

The reduced pressure of the power environment means that

there has been, in some senses, less bureaucracy, especially less centralization. It will be argued later in this chapter that there has occurred at the same time more standardization. These contrary trends are not incompatible. As Corwin has said with reference to the American school system, different aspects of bureaucracy may change independently: 'Centralization, standardization, and specialization do not necessarily occur at the same rates. It is possible for a school system to be highly centralized and yet not standardized or specialized to the same degree.'[17]

As the state began to assume responsibility for elementary education in the middle of the nineteenth century, all the indications were that a national system of schools would be subjected to tight central control. Developments in public education occurred during the Benthamite revolution in public administration; central to this revolution was the 'principle of inspectability' enunciated in *The Constitutional Code*. Kay-Shuttleworth, appointed secretary of the newly formed Committee of Council for Education in 1839, had obtained his experience of public administration as a medical man working under the Benthamite Poor Law. Like Edwin Chadwick he saw inspection and centralization as the cornerstone of efficient public service.

Inspectors were appointed under the Factory Act of 1833 and the Poor Law Act of 1834. By the time the public control of education became an issue, in the eighteen-forties, inspection by the central government was well established, but did not lack critics. Criticism was shrill in the debates which surrounded the Public Health Bill of 1848. The provisions of the bill, said the *Morning Chronicle*, would 'prove galling and intolerable to the English independence of spirit and hatred of perpetual interference'.

And yet, it was after this time that Kay-Shuttleworth applied the Benthamite principle of inspectability most ruthlessly in the field of education. Government inspection was made a condition of all educational grants; indeed, government inspection of schools (and a public code of education) were established before a single school had been built at government expense. Kay-Shuttleworth's centralizing inclinations also find expression in the employment of teachers, whose 'licence to teach' under the regulations of 1846 was properly a licence to secure public money, from central sources, towards their salaries. They were paid an augmentation grant directly by government – although government refused to accept responsibility for them as employees.

Robert Lowe was a decentralizer. His Revised Code of 1862 and the system of 'Payment-by-Results' have significance as a reversal of Kay-Shuttleworth's centralizing measures. The Code abolished augmentation grants and pensions for teachers, and instead provided for a capitation grant to be paid to school managers. 'Thus the direct connection between teachers or pupil-teachers and the state was cut and they were thrown on the mercy of school managers.'[18]

A remote power environment was exchanged for a more immediate and possibly constricting one. School managers have often shown an undue relish for power, even up to the present day. Vicars Bell has recalled his headmastership of a village school in the nineteen-thirties:

> In my village it was the custom of the managers to meet and discuss the affairs of the school without consulting the head or asking him to be present. This was, of course, not an intentional slight, but was part of the dead hand of the past, when schoolmasters were kept in proper subjection.[19]

In fact bureaucratic control over schools, whether by central or local government agencies, has not developed in the way that many feared in the late nineteenth century. The Reports of the Clarendon Commission on the public schools in 1864 and of the Taunton Commission on the endowed schools in 1868 seemed to herald undue interference by government; but the Head Masters' Conference which was established in 1869 and the Head Masters' Association in 1890 were protective alliances which proved to be superfluous defences against the imagined encroachments of central and local authorities. The Board of Education, established in 1902, deliberately contrived that the governing bodies of secondary schools (and H.M.I.s) should themselves constitute important defences against local bureaucracy.

The year 1902, like 1862, may be seen as a landmark in a process of de-bureaucratization. The new Board stressed from the outset the need for secondary schools to enjoy considerable independence through their governing bodies. *The Regulations for Secondary Schools* (1905) claimed:

> experience proves that in a school of the Secondary type full efficiency can be secured and the best teaching and organizational power attracted, only when the Head Master or Head Mistress is entrusted with a large amount of responsibility for and control over teaching, organization and discipline. In particular the appointment and dismissal of Assistant Staff is a matter in which a voice ought to be secured by the Head Master.[20]

Senior officials of the Board of Education (and H.M.I.s) were mainly products of the public schools which they tended to take as models, not only in curricular matters, but in their mode of government. They attempted to secure something of the same independence for maintained secondary schools, and their ally in this (against Directors and Secretaries of Education) was the governing body. Thus, as George Baron has observed, 'it is interesting to note that, from this time, governing bodies were intended to become the protectors of the independence of headmasters of the new secondary schools rather than, as envisaged by the nineteenth-century reformers, the means for checking their excesses.'[21]

Universities have experienced a comparable process of de-bureaucratization – in spite of the obvious rise to power of the University Grants Committee and the growth of internal bureaucracies centred on the vice-chancellor and the registrar.[22] In their case the most important element in their power environment in the past has been the University Council, with its majority of lay members; it is through the council that they have been constrained by society (although often the council has protected them *from* 'society', and has been able to do so effectively on account of the regional and national standing of its members). The recent (1969–1970) furore at the University of Warwick about the council's membership and powers, and its allegedly unnatural alliance with the vice-chancellor,[23] serves merely to illustrate its present-day impotence. The key issue was not the power of council, but its subservience to the vice-chancellor.

Today the University Grants Committee issues what amount to open directives which lay down the general contours of a university's development, its size, rate of growth, and the balance of its academic activities. But often planning committees in universities, perhaps especially in the technological universities and in the new polytechnics, spend a great deal of time guessing what the U.G.C., the D.E.S., and the C.N.A.A. and similar governmental and quasi-governmental bodies, 'really want': they impute power which is not actually there.[24] Often they seem to believe that these authorities are demanding a narrowly vocational and industrial relevance: the technological universities search the Robbins Report to justify not their autonomous behaviour but their adherence to their traditionally 'industrially relevant' curricula. Ritualism is not necessarily a sign of external constraint, but often of the reverse.[25]

The remarkable change that has occurred in university government this century is the decline in the power of the council and the rise in the power of academic staff. Academic self-government is of recent origin. Rowland Eustace has shown that 'general opinion down to the mid-nineteenth century saw no close connection between scholarly activity and control of universities. It is difficult to find so much as a hint of it in the protests against the creation of the University of London in 1836 with nil staff autonomy.'[26]

The nineteenth-century universities were heavily lay-controlled. 'Indeed the need for lay control was urged as a reason for unitary universities. Liverpool's case for a charter rested in part on the fact that the distance to Manchester had practically thrown the business men of Liverpool entirely out of the government of the university.'[27] But there are many indications that lay activity has been diminishing in recent decades, and this is reflected in the instruments of government of recently established universities. 'The shift in emphasis visible in the newer instruments is thus strong evidence that the lay-dominated council has not for a good many years exercised any initiative in university government. In fact, it is clear that councils, as such, play very little part in what is usually thought of as governing at all. . . .'[28] The provincial universities have detached themselves from their provinces; they have evaded what has traditionally been the dominant element in their power environment. At the same time there has been 'a steady and cumulatively massive shift in the direction of academic self-government'.[29]

The formal definition of rights and obligations is insufficient to explain the power relationships within an organization or its power relationships with the wider society. A crucial circumstance is the properties of the members it takes in and the way they define the situation in which they find themselves. A college or school is linked to its environment through its members and the rights and values they bring with them from the wider society. It is not a self-sealing system; its personnel are constantly joining and leaving; it is continuously affected by its input.

An 'action approach' to the study of organizations reinstates the external world. 'Functionalist' and 'systems' approaches have neglected the motivations which 'actors' bring to their work. Industrial sociologists have emphasized in recent years the all-important character of the socio-technical system of the plant. We now have 'two sociologies':[30] the action approach runs the danger of 'psychologism';[31] but the motivations of 'actors' have themselves a social source which accounts for the regularities of social conduct to which they lead.

Lockwood and his associates were unable to account for the behaviour of the affluent industrial workers whom they investigated solely in terms of the 'socio-technical system': thus manual workers and white-collar workers defined the work situation quite differently, they looked for different satisfactions in work, and, while the latter approved of supervisors who were 'friendly' and 'willing to listen', the former liked supervisors who left them alone.[32] Even the 'alienated' attitudes of workers were to be explained principally in terms of their previous social experiences:

> If, therefore, these workers are to be considered as 'alienated', the roots of their alienation must be sought not merely in the technological character of the plants in which they are now employed but, more fundamentally, in those aspects of the wider society which generate their tremendous drive for economic advancement and their disregard for the costs of this through the impoverishment of their working lives.[33]

Similarly Trow and Halsey, in trying to account for the attitudes of university teachers to the authority systems in which they worked, found that their position in the system afforded an inadequate explanation. Of greater importance were the social and political values which they brought with them to their work. Thus those teachers who were 'left' in their general political views favoured democratically controlled departments: 'Proportionately twice as many of the Far Left as of the Right are democrats in their university department....' Attitudes to the distribution of power in universities, which were found in this sample of university teachers, were 'linked to the social and political structure of society as well as to the changing structure of higher education'.[34]

An educational institution will find itself constrained not only by the characteristics of individuals who enter, but by the group characteristics of the intake. Thus changing proportions of male and female, high ability and low ability, working class and middle class pupils will affect the educational arrangements that have to be made. The swing from science creates a serious input problem for science and engineering departments in universities, and is an especially acute embarrassment to the technological universities and the polytechnics. They must compete with more prestigeful and attractive institutions for the inadequate supply of good science sixth-formers. In order to keep up their numbers they will offer hybrid, arts–science courses, hoping to attract good arts sixth-formers who may have some latent leaning towards science and technology. These hybrid courses will be justified according to the loftiest educational principles of 'breadth', 'synthesis', and the 'unity of knowledge'. In fact they are primarily a device to keep the technological universities in business.

The rights that pupils bring with them, as well as their abilities and academic interests, are more relevant to actual power dispositions in schools. When pupils can make a claim to a particular variety of education simply on the basis of their rights as men, they are in a strong position *vis-à-vis* the school authorities. In the light of his extensive American experiences, Jacques Barzun, the President of Columbia University, has written feelingly on the subject of 'instruction without authority'. 'When under democracy education ceases to be a privilege and becomes a right, the student's motive and attitude change. The class turns into a clientele to be satisfied, and a sceptical one: teach me, if you can.' The teacher's relationship with his pupil is 'no longer one of legitimate authority met by willing submission, but one of popularity-seeking met by patronizing tolerance.'³⁵ In these circumstances students' assessments and ratings of their teachers become reasonable as a basis for promotion up the salary and status scale.

When, even in a democratic society, there is 'undemocratic' selectivity for various branches of education, the basis of pupils' rights is quite different: their place in the educational institution is not a right *qua* humanity, inalienable and unalterable; it is provisional and contractual, dependent on the prior and continued demonstration of appropriate abilities.

The comprehensive university which is at the centre of fashionable debate on higher education, open to anyone simply by virtue of his humanity, would probably find itself with the same problems of power as those described by Burton Clark in the 'open-door' American college. Clark relates the system of control or compliance to two variables – selectivity and voluntariness. The open-door college is unselective and voluntary. Clark describes its predicament in the following terms:

> When students pass the age of compulsory school attendance, usually at 16, the relation between students and the school changes. . . . If [the student] also has the right to enter a non-selective college, then his voluntariness becomes an active force. He can decide for himself whether and when he will enter and actively contend for his own version of the ends and means of his education. The conjunction of non-selection and age above compulsory schooling in the public junior college gives maximum thrust to the choices and characteristics of students.³⁶

The open-door college finds itself 'at the point in the educational structure where professional dictation is likely to be minimal'.

> As a consequence of dependency on an unselective-voluntary clientele, such a college will be extensively shaped by characteristics of the multitude. Of all types of school, the unselective-voluntary type will be most open to wide clientele influence.³⁷

The way of handling and moderating 'student thrust' in the American open-door college is through counselling, which the majority of staff regard as being at least as important as teaching. But if staff insist on their professional goals and fail to persuade their students to accept them through counselling, the alternative is coercion. Voluntary students may, of course, withdraw if they find coercion unpalatable; but if they value the qualifications that are offered they will be inclined to stay. And this is the danger of 'open', voluntary and unselective education after the age of compulsory schooling: that it will be more coercive and not less. The voluntary but selective English sixth-forms and universities that we have known have been generally tolerant, humane and relaxed in their pupil–staff relationships. They are likely to become tyrannical as they are democratized – if staff are so foolish as to insist on the attainment of goals and standards which they have always cherished.

In 1922 Atkinson, the headmaster of Oundle, was asked by the governors to resign because it had come to light that he had been looking for a job elsewhere.[38] The attribute of the staff 'input' that is still crucial to power relations in schools is loyalty. The reference which makes no mention of the applicant's loyal service over the past fifteen years is unlikely to be taken seriously.

The relationship between professional men and the organization that employs them has often been discussed in terms of the distinction between 'locals' and 'cosmopolitans'. Locals differ from cosmopolitans in a variety of important ways; but crucially they differ in organizational loyalty. The cosmopolitan is far more likely than the local to take off if attractive opportunities present themselves elsewhere, regardless of all other considerations.

Merton's original formulation of the distinction between locals and cosmopolitans arose from his study of preferences among the influential citizens of Rovere for newspapers of different emphasis and scope. A broad distinction could be drawn between those with strong local interests and involvements, and those with wider horizons and 'reference groups'. The former were strongly identified with the locality and generally felt that the folk of the town were the salt of the earth; the latter – who had often, though not invariably, enjoyed more formal education and had lived in a succession of communities – were more guarded and circumspect in their judgement of their fellow townsmen.[39]

Merton's work on a residential community has been interestingly transposed to studies of members of formal organizations. In work situations locals (or organizationals) tend to be 'company men', loyal to the organization which employs them, placing high value on the good opinion of their superiors in the firm, and seeking their advancement in that firm. Cosmopolitans (or professionals) have a different loyalty – to their fellow professionals wherever they may be. They seek a wider reputation; they accept the discipline of their peers rather than of their organizational superiors.

Both American and British sociologists have examined the functioning of locals and cosmopolitans in various work situations – in universities, social work agencies,[40] and scientific laboratories.[41] (In industrial production the sharp contrast between 'staff' and 'line' appears to correspond loosely to the distinction between cosmopolitans and locals: production managers are not only more stable and involved in the firm than research and development men; they are generally less highly qualified in a formal, academic sense, and they are more restricted in their social, intellectual and cultural interest.[42]) In general, people with the highest qualifications tend to be cosmopolitan (and disloyal); they fret at the constraints of bureaucracy which requires for its functioning loyalty and dedication to its goals. The sharp distinction between locals and cosmopolitans (or organizationals and professionals) has been questioned in recent research.[43] Nevertheless, there is probably a predisposition for a man to be *either* local *or* cosmopolitan in his outlook, according to the type of education he has received and perhaps according to various social experiences and aspects of personality.

With regard to educational institutions, studies of loyalty have been heavily concentrated on universities. The dedicated scientist or scholar in the university is generally loyal to the institutional goals of science and scholarship (the furtherance of knowledge and the production of published research) rather than to organizational goals (teaching and the production of graduates). The attachment of such men is to 'invisible colleges' of fellow scientists throughout the world. They are frequently on circuit; 'they then return to home base, but always their allegiance is to the group rather than to the institution which supports them, unless it happens to be a station on such a circuit'.[44] In their studies of America's 'academic market-place', Caplow and McGee have concluded that

Today, a scholar's orientation to his institution is apt to disorient him to his discipline and to affect his professional prestige unfavorably. Conversely, an orientation to his discipline will disorient him to his institution, which he will regard as a temporary shelter where he can pursue his career as a member of the discipline.[45]

Clearly such circumstances raise serious problems for the distribution of power and authority in universities: 'Power cannot, therefore, be tied to specific positions in the form of authority....' A man in a particular rank may not have commensurate external prestige. The American solution, we are told, is 'to let power lodge pretty much where it may'.[46]

English academics' attitudes to power and authority in their universities have also been related to their local–cosmopolitan orientations. Cosmopolitans are inclined to see their rank as an acknowledgement by the university of their external prestige. Such men would moderate the rigours of the organizational power structure. In particular they would weaken professorial power. And 'Within categories of political position, cosmopolitan orientations continue to show a strong relation to "democratic" attitudes towards the Professorship.'[47] They, too, would probably be inclined to let power lodge pretty much where it may.

If an educational institution recruits cosmopolitans rather than locals, the stress within the formal power structure is likely to be considerable. Cosmopolitans are likely to be independent in their attitudes, resistant to bureaucratic control. They will challenge the decisions and directives of principals and heads of department with reference to external standards and practices. There is even a danger, as Gouldner has suggested in a general discussion of these issues, that 'organizational survival may be threatened by a recruiting policy which attends solely to the expertise of the candidate', since well-qualified experts tend to be cosmopolitan in outlook.[48] A shrewd headmaster or principal – or one interested in maintaining his power – may thus be tempted, from time to time, to appoint the least qualified candidate for a post; his loyalty will be less in doubt.

The power implications of recruitment policies will be seen most clearly when an educational institution like a technical college, which has been essentially local in its composition, transforms itself into a university and is tempted to recruit cosmopolitans. If it wishes to preserve the autocratic power of the principal and the due subjection of its social science departments to service teaching for engineers, it will be unwise to recruit its registrar and its professors from traditional universities. The situation is likely to resemble circumstances described by Riesman in America:

> the home-guard are typically concerned with the university's service functions to students and to the locale, rather than with research and with participation in the national intellectual life ... the itinerant cosmopolitans bring with them ... a more elitist conception of academia which emphasizes a small but select student body and a research-oriented curriculum....[49]

They may have a distressing habit of referring to what happens in 'a proper university'.

Schools do not necessarily face the same dilemma, or so acute a dilemma, as universities. A good schoolmaster may be an expert at his job in its manifold aspects both inside and outside the classroom, in spite of, or perhaps because of, his 'local' orientations. Some types of school probably have a strong attraction, and an equally strong preference, for men (and women) with pronounced 'local' inclinations. Wakeford has shown how, in a public boarding school, staff are deeply immersed in their local world,[50] and as servants of this particular type of community, are probably all the more effective for their total immersion. The 'cosmopolitan' schoolmaster has a less obvious and well-organized external universe to support his wider interests, pretensions and commitments. He may become involved in professional and subject associations; he may write textbooks or publicize new teaching methods and apparatus. Such possibilities are probably increasing. But his opportunities for external fame are fewer than a professor's. Comparatively few schoolmasters will acquire such prestige on a wider stage as will overawe the headmaster. (Professors have been known to overawe vice-chancellors, and assistant lecturers, professors.)

Kob's research into teachers in Germany led him to distinguish between two types – one essentially interested in an academic subject and finding much of his satisfaction in life outside school in literary and cultural pursuits; the other interested primarily in teaching skills, the management of boys, and non-school activities which still involved young people.[51] But there is nothing in Kob's study to suggest that the former are more 'disloyal' than the latter. Indeed, whereas the issue of loyalty has been at the heart of the difference between locals and cosmopolitans in universities, research laboratories, and social work agencies, it may be irrelevant to the distinction in the school situation. The position in schools is not strictly comparable and is probably more complex. Nurses with a strong professional commitment have been found not to be low on loyalty to their hospitals, but unusually high.[52] The same may be true of teachers, and for the same reason – the non-public nature of their expertise.

Toomey's recent factor-analytical study of the values of a group of English teachers taking higher degrees shows the dangers of applying a simplistic local–cosmopolitan distinction to the school situation. It is true that Toomey found the familar local–cosmopolitan differences with respect to preferences for teaching rather than research and the value placed on reputation among immediate colleagues compared with professional colleagues in the wider world. But the main indicator of 'loyalty' used in other studies – the preference for promotion within one's present organization rather than through preferment elsewhere – was not a distinguishing characteristic; neither was the inclination to look for a more powerful position.

But Toomey extracted a second 'factor' which seems to represent the ambitious teacher who will pursue his own career interests regardless of the consequences for his present school. This factor is 'closely connected with ambitiousness [and] is independent of a factor which approximates to the conventional local–cosmopolitan distinction.' Toomey comments as follows:

> But the second factor suggests that 'local–cosmopolitan' differences are not uni-dimensional. For the second factor appears to refer to ambitiousness, desire to lead, desire for economic security and tolerance of competitiveness. It corresponds to a choice between management on the one hand and teaching or

research on the other. The choice seems to approximate to a choice between the go-ahead, driving manager or administrator, ambitious to get on, ready to compete, desirous of leadership, and the retiring academic who prefers secure and assured economic rewards, advancing knowledge rather than producing results, relying on superiors rather than leading others, and preferring promotion within the organization in which he is known.[53]

The recruitment of management-oriented teachers of this type is likely to have more significance for power relationships in schools than the recruitment of 'cosmopolitans'. While they will tend to regard the school as a temporary halt on the upward path of promotion, they will in due course expect loyalty from their own subordinates.

Conceivably schools set more store by staff loyalty than other contemporary bureaucracies. Crozier maintains that the broad historical trend is for large-scale bureaucracies to become less bureaucratic in the severity of their control over members. Formerly, 'Whether they were employees of the Fugger House, members of the Jesuit order, or Prussian grenadiers, they had to devote themselves completely to the organization. Leaving it was equivalent to treason....' A modern organization can tolerate more deviance and demand only temporary commitments. Relaxation has been notable even over the past thirty years: 'Compare, for example, the discipline and conformity of dress and behaviour imposed on the sales force of a large department store today with the standards of thirty years ago – a great deal more was required then, and in a much harsher way.'[54] If schools are to come into line with the tempered bureaucracies that Crozier describes, a teacher who looks for another job even within one or two years of appointment, should not have to feel that he is committing a treasonable offence.

A standardized output, no less than a recalcitrant input, influences the power relations within a school. And it links the school in a characteristic way with society. Both because it is standard and because it is years in the making, the product is insensitive to market conditions; the market must accommodate itself to the product.

But in the long run it is the nature of the market, our modern highly mobile society, with its need for interchangeable (and therefore standard) parts, that determines the standardization of education. Replacements for those who move on must be a ready fit. And standard parts are most appropriately produced in hierarchical, rule-regulated, mechanistic organizations, whether educational or industrial.

Sociologists who are also educationists are usually unwilling to concede that schools are bureaucracies, because they lay emphasis on the non-standard character of educational products and procedures[55] (though they may concede that the Weberian model fits the school *system* quite well[56]). Thus Grambs maintains:

> The school as an organizational system can never approximate Weber's model.... Personnel in the school system are continually making new decisions about unique events (people); the school is staffed by persons with the same job title (teacher) but with greatly varying ability to develop a product which is never standard....[57]

And it is true that a school's product (whether for other schools, universities, or the wider society) cannot be standardized in the same, literal, sense as machine parts. To describe schools as 'people-processing' doubtless suggests that the raw material is more inert and malleable than is actually the case. Idiosyncrasy, even downright perversity, from time to time breaks through.

But the school of the last fifty years is remarkable on any broad historical or comparative perspective for its standardized procedures and practices. The camera has provided us with vivid visual evidence of the rapid process of standardization in the closing decades of the nineteenth century. In 1912 Arthur Ponsonby considered that the public schools were turning out a stereotyped product, in sharp contrast to forty or fifty years previously. Organized, compulsory games (bitterly opposed by Moberly at Winchester, and by other headmasters who were correctly reading the signs of the times) were now as general as the school certificate examinations. Ponsonby pointed to the variety of attire and posture in photographs of mid-nineteenth-century football teams: boys were 'lounging about in different attitudes with a curious variety of costumes'. But by 1912:

> The group of today consists of two or three rows of boys beautifully turned out with immaculate, perfectly fitting clothing.... They stand and sit so that the line of the peaks of their caps, of their folded arms, and their bare knees, is mathematically level. And even their faces! You can hardly tell one from another.

Ponsonby took this as 'an outward and visible sign not only of the love of the appearance of smartness, but of the stereotyping and conventionalizing effect of our modern educational system. This stereotyping constitutes perhaps the strongest indictment that has to be brought against our Public Schools.'[58] Ponsonby placed the blame mainly on the new system of public examinations,[59] then only some thirty or forty years old. The upshot was that 'We set up an iron mould and we purposely and intentionally stamp out and bake the soft clay into a fixed pattern. We sacrifice individuality and suppress originality so as to produce a conventional average type.'[60]

Over the same period the system of 'payment-by-results' had ruthlessly standardized the elementary school product. The Revised Code of 1862 was a measure of decentralization; it was also a signal measure of standardization. School classes were now known as 'standards'. Educational practice was defined in a code (which did not finally disappear until 1944, forty-six years after the financial arrangements of payment-by-results).

Ponsonby was not the first to attack educational standardization – and he was certainly not the last. Small-group work, individual work, projects, discovery methods, the Dalton Plan, Nuffield science, flexible curricula, new-type – even open-book – examinations have all been tried to counteract standardization and uniformity. The Board of Education turned its official face against standardization in the 1918 edition of the *Handbook of Suggestions for the Consideration of Teachers*:

> The only uniformity of practice that the Board of Education desire to see in the teaching of public elementary schools is that

each teacher shall think for himself, and work out for himself such methods of teaching as may use his powers to the best advantage and be best suited to the particular needs and conditions of the school. Uniformity in detail of practice (except in the mere routine of school management) is not desirable, even if it were attainable.

The authors of the Plowden Report on primary schools were not the first to point out how difficult it was in practice for teachers to take advantage of such theoretical freedoms.[61] And the underlying reason is this: that complex and highly developed societies like our own, which are also remarkable for their high rates of mobility, require not only attested standards of competence – qualifications which have a universal currency; they also require readily interchangeable parts. When people leave their employers, they must be replaced so that the change is barely noticed. Indeed, the relaxation with respect to bureaucratic loyalty, to which Crozier has drawn our attention, is possible only because we have more bureaucratization in the sense of job and employee standardization. The schools are the servants of this over-riding social requirement.

The product of our schools is not typically uncertain and unpredictable in the same way that the product of a scientific research laboratory must always be in doubt. Nor is it necessarily variable in the same way that the bespoken output of unit production arises from special orders for unique products. Neither the research laboratory nor the firm engaged in unit production is able to function with the hierarchical order and set procedures of mass-production factories and schools. No school or university would respond favourably to the client who placed an order for a brace of young men in two or three years' time who had a grasp of the Japanese economy, a command of the Japanese language, and a sensitivity and adaptability to unusual cultural conditions (especially when the next client might want a brace of equally enterprising computer-programmers with a deep knowledge of crop fertilization). Partly by denying the propriety of the consumer to place specific orders; and partly because of the requirements of long-term educational planning, schools place themselves in a special relationship with their market. Like the modern corporations described by Galbraith,[62] they must create rather than respond to demand; and appointments officers are faced with the problem of persuading Fine Fare and the police force that their needs will be admirably met from the current abundance of history graduates.

Joan Woodward[63] has shown in her examination of more than a hundred Essex firms how power and authority in an organization are distributed and exercised according to the type of production. Unit production, mass production and highly automatic process production varied in the type of organization they required; and they varied in their relationship with their markets. In unit production the first job of management was to find an order; in mass production development came first; in process production the pilot stage came first. Both the relationship with the market and the system of production were closely related to the type of authority structure that prevailed. Unit production corresponds most closely to the educational ideal, low in authoritarianism, high in personal interaction and consultation, with development and innovation built in to the process of production. Mass production corresponds more closely to educational reality: with considerable pressure from superiors, little consultation, and research and development carried out by specialists cut off from the business of front-line production.

The type of output is a crucial distinguishing feature of the ideal-type (and actual) authority systems described by Burns and Stalker: the 'mechanistic' and the 'organic'. In mechanistic systems hierarchy is emphasized, powers and duties attached to each functional role are precisely defined; and operations are governed by decisions and instructions of supervisors. And such a system – as Burns and Stalker found, for instance, in a rayon mill – works well under constant production conditions and relatively unchanging market demand. A clear line of command, close definition of jobs, and generally authoritarian control, are seen as reasonable by members, and constitute an efficient system, under stable conditions. In organic systems hierarchy is de-emphasized, necessary action cannot be broken down and distributed among specialist roles, jobs and statuses are loosely defined and continually redefined. And such a system – as found, for instance, in a technologically progressive and innovative electronics firm – is appropriate to unstable conditions of production and a constantly changing market, where 'every contract required some special units and there was a constant flow of design improvements'.[64] A clearly defined hierarchy is dysfunctional in uncertainty 'which gives rise constantly to fresh problems and unforeseen requirements for action....'[65]

In organic systems there is flexibility, adaptability – and chronic anxiety. No one is sure how to behave towards anyone else, because 'nobody here is very clear about his title or status, or even his function'. (In the electronics firm 'It was claimed that nobody on the staff had a title except the managing director.') The tendency is to revert to mechanical systems, even though they may be inappropriate, mainly because they are more comfortable: people 'know where they stand'.

But there is an interaction between the personality-type – or at least the general value-systems – of organizational members and the organizational structure. A 'cosmopolitan' orientation is congruent with organic, a 'local' orientation with mechanistic systems.[66] Studies of managers' attitudes to the introduction of computer systems for administrative purposes have indicated that 'cosmopolitan' managers in organic firms are likely to be more positive in their attitudes to change, innovative and adventurous, than 'locals' in mechanistic organizations. The value-orientations and the type of organization are mutually reinforcing. The 'local' finds assurance in his rule-regulated environment and sees innovation as threatening.[67]

Education which caters for a stable market and produces an unvarying, standardized product will be well served by 'locals' in 'mechanistic' organizations. Members of a research unit, or of a university postgraduate department, producing a non-standard and even unpredictable output for a changing market, will be ill served by such men and such systems. The difficulties in changing from one organizational form to another are formidable, because it is not only a question of changing formal arrangements, but men's values and attitudes. Thus to change a technical college (staffed mainly by 'locals' and geared to a standard product for a stable market) into a university dedicated to producing non-standard graduates and postgraduates for innovative work in unforeseen circumstances (especially when they are still tied to a relatively stable and predictable market through their sandwich courses) is virtually impossible – without a massive infusion of cosmopolitans into senior posts. A charter and other apparatus of organizational change will not alter the values and orientations of those already in post.

ORGANIZATIONAL AND PERSONALITY DIMENSIONS IN EDUCATION

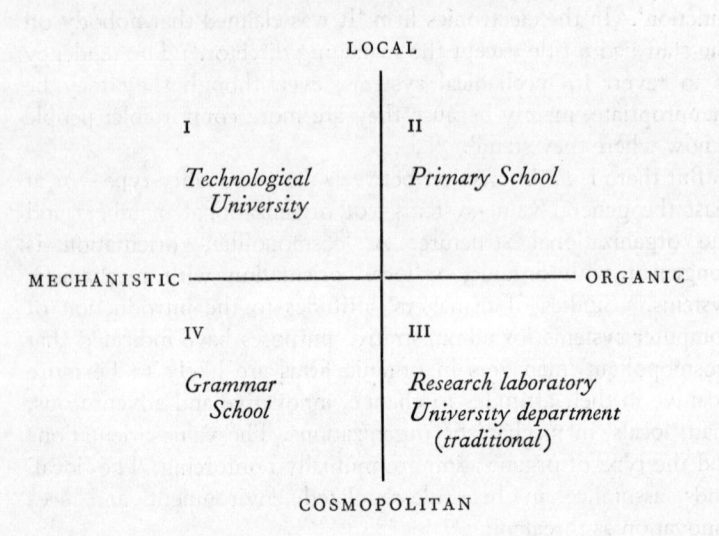

	LOCAL	
	I	II
	Technological University	*Primary School*
MECHANISTIC		ORGANIC
	IV	III
	Grammar School	*Research laboratory University department (traditional)*
	COSMOPOLITAN	

CELL

I   High on authoritarianism and hierarchy
    Low on innovation

II Moderate on authoritarianism and hierarchy
    Moderate on innovation

III Low on authoritarianism and hierarchy
    High on innovation

IV Moderate on authoritarianism and hierarchy
    Moderate on innovation

Organizations in Cell I are the antithesis of those in Cell III: they are hierarchical, authoritarian, non-innovative, with a standard product for a stable market; and in consequence uncertainty in their operations is minimal. And in this circumstance lies their inferiority and lack of power. Behaviour which is programmed, routinized, predictable – is underpowered behaviour: 'the predictability of one's behaviour is the sure test of one's inferiority'.[68] Organizations which produce predictable, standard products are in a weak bargaining position *vis-à-vis* the consumer. As Crozier observes: 'As long as the requirements of action create conditions of uncertainty, the individuals who have to face them have power over those who are affected by the results of their choice.'[69] The trend towards standardization in education over the past century is at the root of its decline in power. It has ceased either to astonish or dismay. It has lost its power in producing interchangeable and highly predictable ('reliable') parts.

10 Power, the future and the counter-culture

One might hope that the examination of power and authority in education presented in this book would soon be utterly irrelevant – at least by the end of the century. This would be the hope of any self-respecting anarchist, indeed, of any self-respecting humanist. By the end of the century, conceivably, automation will have eliminated scarcity and the need for power; and we can all then be artists, exactly as William Morris would have wished. Neo-anarchists like Herbert Marcuse and all the prophets of the Californian counter-culture are pointing the way. Headmasters – and constraints and boundaries of every kind – will wither away. Abundance will make schools as superfluous as power.

This book has argued the need to increase the power of schools if they are to attain their goals. But these goals may soon be pointless. Any goals for schools may soon be pointless. And there are other reasons for this than a possibly imminent cyberculture. It is not only Liam Hudson who holds the view that 'much of what passes for education in this country and the United States is a waste of everybody's time, pupils and teachers alike'.[1] It may be an important function of schools, though it is scarcely a goal, to do precisely this – to waste the time of young people who have become socially and economically redundant.[2] Such time wasting might be done more enjoyably, profitably and cheaply by other means.

But even in relation to educational goals which are relevant to the maintenance of our present socio-economic order, schools as we know them may be clumsy, obsolescent, and unfair. These goals may be more effectively and justly pursued out of schools than in them. Schools with clearly defined boundaries which mark them off from society, encompassing and protective environments for the young, made good sense when the world was by definition evil and contaminating. Monks and Puritans defined the world in these terms: and so did Rousseau, whose educational proposals were equally socially evasive. In the post-Mayo era even factories are benign. The school takes on the appearance of an intellectually impoverished and socially deprived environment, stunting the development of the young, cutting them off from all vital and truly educative experiences whatsoever – especially opportunities for responsible, productive action. It is no longer essential or particularly important as a source of knowledge in societies now remarkable for their information pluralism: society produces and purveys information on a scale and with a force that no school can match.[3]

'The idea that the only way people get education is by being enrolled in institutions is long obsolete.'[4] In a controversial (and officially suppressed) Unesco document, Huberman has pointed to some of the implications of this circumstance, the consequences for education 'when fixed cycles of attendance are replaced by intermittent leaving and re-entry: when facilities for education are available outside institutions of learning'. When every child has been issued with his educational coupon, he will buy his education not only in the schools of his choice, but in other approved organizations where accredited experiences are to be obtained. The school is then a clearing house, a co-ordinating mechanism; teachers phase and perhaps integrate a rich variety of educative episodes. Life becomes one vast sandwich course.

There are those, especially in the technological universities, who would see this as a consummation devoutly to be wished. But even this degree of contrivance and control may be rendered unnecessary. In a cybernetic future of material abundance, which self-regulating, even self-improving production systems will ensure, traditional socio-economic roles will no longer need to be filled. All will be play. Society will become 'a brotherhood of clowns'.[5] This is a consummation even more devoutly to be wished than an endless sandwich course. Power and the Protestant Ethic which gives it sanctity or camouflage are central targets of the counter-culture.[6] Just as Shelley, Godwin, Coleridge and Wordsworth in his youth attacked them in the early phases of industrialization; so they are the focus of attack in the early phases of post-industrial society. (One minor difference between the two movements is that opium has been superseded by pot.)

The counter-culture supports the values of sincerity and authenticity. At its centre is a quest for purity. Its most general term of abuse is 'garbage'. Whatever is contaminated, corrupt or spurious is subsumed under this term. It extols naturalism, emotion rather than reason, art (including handicraft), and mutual aid. It approves mind-expanding drugs but rejects alcohol. In its extreme form it leads to bucolic retreatism. But above all it is against bureaucracy and power, and especially the 'military-industrial complex'. It is also against more personal forms of 'exchange-power'; sex is not manipulative – hence the injunction to sleep with a stranger. It feeds on astrology, numerology, Eastern philosophy (and the music of the Beatles). It pervades the American university campus. The young and the not-so-young wander barefoot in the park playing on their flutes. It has many of the characteristics of a demanding extra-curriculum, which is perhaps more attuned and sensitive to the changing needs and character of society than the intra-curriculum. It suggests a form of anticipatory socialization for the cyberculture which, in California at least, may be just around the corner. It flowers in the shadow that the automated future casts before it. It is unusual in being a form of deviant behaviour associated with the affluent and socially privileged rather than the poor and underprivileged. It is the curriculum for the new leisure class.

In fact, all the indications are that its tuning is faulty and its anticipations misplaced. The prognostications of Robert Theobald[7] never mature into more than half-truths. Galbraith has pointed out that the average work week in American manufacturing industry was longer in 1965 (41.1 hours) than in 1941 (40.6 hours) and rising;[8] that in any case work is more pleasant than it was, and 'With more pleasant work and expanded wants, a man is somewhat more likely to choose more work than more leisure.' Men in senior, responsible, professional professions have still less leisure:

As one moves into and up through the technostructure, men increasingly exercise the option of more work and more income. And some pride themselves on an unlimited and competitive commitment to toil.... It follows that to argue for less work and more leisure, as a natural goal of industrial man, is to misread the character of the industrial system.[9]

Somewhat more laboriously, and infinitely more obscurely, Herbert Marcuse makes essentially the same point in his more recent writings. Power persists because 'one-dimensional man' is persuaded that he wants more goods. This is a pity, because in his optimism in the nineteen-fifties, when he wrote *Eros and Civilization*, Marcuse saw power, with its origins in scarcity, withering away in a world of abundance. Even love would cease to be dominative, phallic, and would be diffused more widely over the erogenous zones: genital supremacy would be superseded by the eroticization of the entire personality. Marcuse made a distinction between 'basic repression' which any functioning social system requires, and 'surplus repression' required by all historical forms of economic production.[10] But automation brought about unprecedented possibilities. ('Technology operates against the repressive utilization of energy insofar as it minimizes the time necessary for the production of the necessities of life, thus saving time for the development of needs beyond the realm of necessity and of necessary waste.'[11]) Marcuse was wrong. By the nineteen-sixties he recognized that his faith in technology was entirely misplaced:

> The distinguishing feature of advanced industrial society is its effective suffocation of those needs which demand liberation – liberation also from that which is tolerable and rewarding and comfortable – while it sustains and absolves the destructive power and repressive function of the affluent society.[12]

The next two or three decades are likely to be less cataclysmic, socially and technologically speaking, than once seemed likely. The problems of power and authority discussed in this book will remain. We shall still have schools trying to change resistant pupils in particular ways. But the exercise of power is likely to be more problematical for three reasons: the first is that power, though as necessary as ever, will be progressively de-authorized by the ideology of the more widely pervasive counter-culture; the second is that positions of power will be ever less attractive to people of ability; and the third is that even less attractive people than usual will want them. The problem of recruiting headmasters – or anyway, suitable headmasters – and other senior personnel into the educational system may become acute.

The alternative to a position of power and importance is no longer starvation; the marginal advantages of a power position are reduced in a world in which wealth is more equally distributed. While change in the near future may not be cataclysmic, it will be such as to undermine some of our unquestioned certainties – for instance, that social stratification is an effective incentive system. Other forms of reward than high formal status are available, for instance fame through the mass media, obtained without taking on power positions (and authorized by the values of the counter-culture). And power in egalitarian societies is ever more boring, unspectacular, undramatic, muted in its style, cautious, circumspect, exercised in committees. Even great headmasters are now like Snow's men of power, walking briskly down corridors carrying folders of papers, allowed to deal in fairness, never in generosity.[13]

Galbraith has observed the growing difficulty of recruiting to the upper reaches of bureaucratic organizations:

> Ultimately one of the problems of the industrial system may be in reproducing the technostructure. And there may already be signs of difficulty. Once the schools of business, the most general training ground for the technostructure, were among the most prestigious branches of American higher education. They are so no longer.... The best schools have ceased to expect to recruit the best students. And good students, when asked about business, are increasingly adverse. They hold it to be excessively disciplined, damaging to individuality, not worth the high pay, or dull.[14]

And power is made less attractive by power-holders when opportunities for advancement are relatively open. When Keate at Eton in 1832, though in his sixtieth year, exceeded even his usual form by flogging eighty boys in a single day, he was exercising a relatively wholesome power. The Puritan divines of New England in the eighteenth century are only one of countless power groups, high in social prestige, that might be thought to have wrought greater misery. As Ruth Benedict has pointed out:

> Few prestige groups in any culture have been allowed such complete intellectual and emotional dictatorship as they were. They were the voice of God. Yet to a modern observer it is they, not the confused and tormented women they put to death as witches, who were the psycho-neurotics of New England.

And still today, lawyers and businessmen may engage in actions which are 'more asocial than those of the inmates of penitentiaries'. Yet their behaviour is 'supported by every tenet of our civilization'.[15]

Power and power-holders have seldom lacked stern critics. But careers open to talent are likely to attract men who have not only a strong desire for power, but a strong need for it. Russell pointed out this obvious danger:

> Where no social institution, such as aristocracy or hereditary monarchy, exists to limit the number of men to whom power is possible, those who most desire power are, broadly speaking, those most likely to acquire it. It follows that, in a social system in which power is open to all, the posts which confer power will, as a rule, be occupied by men who differ from the average in being exceptionally power loving.[16]

The danger in modern organizations such as schools is less that lusty men of power find their way to senior posts, than that insecure men do so, seeking in positions of authority a prop for their frailties. The danger is not from strong men, but from weak. It is such men, whose quest is for self-assurance, who are most likely to drive their subordinates with obsessive and unintelligent persistence; and to be looking anxiously over their shoulders at their own superiors. They overwork themselves and everyone else. Argyris has described such a leader:

> There is a growing body of evidence to suggest that an ever-active, hard-working leader who keeps his subordinates close to

him tends to have an uncomplimentary picture of himself. This feeling is hardly ever conscious. Because of this type of 'insecurity', he tends to be upset by criticism, no matter how well he 'covers up' with a smile. According to this view, the overwork and constant activity are due to the fact that such a person desires to make a superb record, thereby guaranteeing him success and the resulting praise from his fellow men. This, in turn, minimizes any chance of failure, which would tend to affect him deeply.[17]

Schools probably find their headmasters in large measure from among such men. The problem in open recruitment is to distinguish between men who are primarily interested in performing a task, and those who are primarily concerned to shore up their personal deficiencies.

The problems of power in education are likely to remain as they have been presented in this book. It is improbable that they will be solved or rendered obsolete in the foreseeable future by the advent of the cyberculture. The problem will remain the central one raised by this book: not the reduction of power, but its expansion. This can be done in the various ways already indicated, for instance through internal restructuring of schools which gives more authority positions, to correspond with actual power, within a carefully defined division of labour. But above all expansion of power will come from a fundamental re-ordering of the school's relationship with its environment. Teachers must be able to make significant decisions about this relationship, notably about the characteristics of the school's input and output (including even its age). While it produces a standardized product its power is limited, its bargaining position weak. But perhaps most important are fiscal decisions which must lie with the headmaster and his senior colleagues, including decisions relating to expansion and contraction and marketing the product. Contemporary research reveals the impotence of schools, their widespread failure to attain their goals. But it is also clear that they have not yet been effectively mobilized for their task.

Notes

CHAPTER ONE

1 R. S. Peters, *Authority, Responsibility and Education* (Allen and Unwin, London, 1959) p. 21.
2 Ralf Dahrendorf, *Class and Class Conflict in Industrial Society* (Routledge and Kegan Paul 1967) p. 166.
3 Cf. Talcott Parsons, 'On the Concept of Political Power', *Proceedings of the American Philosophical Society* (1963) vol. 107.
4 Elliott Jaques, *The Changing Culture of a Factory* (Tavistock Publicaations, London, 1951) p. 255.
5 Cf. T. H. Marshall, 'Reflections on Power', *Sociology* (1969) vol. 3.
6 Ralf Dahrendorf, op. cit., p. 166.
7 Basil Bernstein, 'Education Cannot Compensate for Society', *New Society*, 26 February 1970.
8 Ralf Dahrendorf, op. cit., p. 296.
9 Basil Bernstein, 'Open Schools, Open Society', *New Society*, 14 September 1967.
10 Basil Bernstein, 'Sociological Aspects of Classifying and Framing of Educational Knowledge': a paper presented to the annual conference of the British Sociological Association, Durham, 1970.
11 See F. Musgrove, 'The Contribution of Sociology to the Study of the Curriculum' in J. F. Kerr (ed.), *Changing the Curriculum* (University of London Press, London, 1968).
12 M. F. D. Young, 'Curricula and the Social Organization of Knowledge': a paper presented to the annual conference of the British Sociological Association, Durham, 1970.
13 Edward Shils, 'The Intellectuals I. Great Britain', *Encounter*, April 1955.

14 P. Collison and J. Millen, 'University Chancellors, Vice-Chancellors and College Principals: A Social Profile', *Sociology* (1969) vol. 3. Important positions in different sectors of the national life are held either simultaneously or successively: 'Lord Franks may be cited as an example: academic, civil servant, ambassador, bank chairman and academic leader once more.'
15 See Eric Hutchinson, 'Scientists as an Inferior Class', *Minerva* (1970) vol. 8.
16 Eric Ashby, *Technology and the Academics* (Macmillan, London, 1963) p. 66.
17 M. Spiers, 'The Young Technologist, Politics and Society', *Technologist* (1965) vol. 2.
18 F. Musgrove, 'Social Class and Levels of Aspiration in a Technological University', *Sociological Review* (1967) vol. 15, and 'Self Concepts and Occupational Identities', *Universities Quarterly* (1969) vol. 23.
19 F. Musgrove, 'A Widening Gap between Students of Science and Arts', *Educational Research* (1971) forthcoming.
20 E. Gross, 'The Definition of Organizational Goals', *British Journal of Sociology* (1969) vol. 20.
21 See A. W. Gouldner, 'Organizational Analysis' in R. K. Merton (ed.), *Sociology Today* (Basic Books, New York, 1959).
22 E. Gross, loc. cit.
23 M. Albrow, 'The Study of Organizations – Objectivity or Bias?' in Julius Gould (ed.), *Penguin Social Sciences Survey 1968* (Penguin Books, Harmondsworth, 1968).
24 See F. Musgrove and P. H. Taylor, *Society and the Teacher's Role* (Routledge and Kegan Paul, London, 1969) pp. 43–57, and Schools' Council: *Enquiry I. Young School Leavers* (H.M.S.O., 1968).
25 See E. Gross, loc. cit. In a study of the goals of American universities, less than half of the stated goals were output goals.
26 F. Musgrove and P. H. Taylor, op. cit., pp. 58–67.
27 See G. T. Page, *Engineering Among the Schools* (Institution of Mechanical Engineers, 1965).
28 Cf. F. Musgrove, 'Education and the Culture Concept', *Africa* (1953) vol. 23.
29 Marjorie Reeves, 'The European Universities from Medieval Times' in W. R. Niblett (ed.), *Higher Education: Demand and Response* (Tavistock Publications, London, 1969).

These extra-curricular developments occurred at Oxford and Cambridge after the mid-sixteenth century 'educational revolution' which saw the end of the universities as professional schools for training canon lawyers. The universities now provided not training, but a humanist education; their curricular goals were dissociated from clearly defined social needs. The view that the new curriculum represented 'modernization', offering a training for secular careers in court administration, has been effectively criticized by Hugh Kearney. There simply were not the jobs at court for the rising numbers that attended the universities; nor were a few years spent in a college in a small country town like Oxford an obvious path to success:

> If men did flock to the universities in such large numbers it was hardly the chance of becoming a crown official that attracted them. Even if state offices had been more plentiful, it was by no means clear, on the assumptions of the sixteenth century, that a university education offered the best approach to them.

See Hugh Kearney, *Scholars and Gentlemen* (Faber, London, 1970) p. 25. A social function of a post-Reformation university education, as distinct from its curricular goals, was to transform yeoman and merchant families into gentry. Other routes were available (e.g. the army and the court), but a year or two at the university was the easiest and cheapest (p. 27). The selection and organization of knowledge at Oxford and Cambridge did not reflect the values of the dominant power group at court; indeed, the values of the court and of the university were antithetical:

> There were, it would seem, two systems of education, that of the court and that of the universities, each with their own code of values, the one based upon the traditional code of honour and loyalty to one's patron, the other based on a system of religious and academic values (p. 26).

CHAPTER TWO

1 Reported in *The Times Educational Supplement* (Scotland) 24 July 1970, p. 14.
2 For a discussion of 'congruent compliance systems' see A. Etzioni, *Complex Organizations* (Free Press of Glencoe, Illinois, 1961) pp. 6–16.
3 C. Wright Mills, *The Sociological Imagination* (Oxford University Press, New York, 1959) p. 40.
4 Ibid., p. 40.

5 A. W. Astin, 'Undergraduate Achievement and Institutional Excellence', *Science* (1968) vol. 161.
6 J. W. B. Douglas, *The Home and the School* (MacGibbon and Kee, London, 1964) pp. 108–11.
7 Central Advisory Council for Education, *Children and their Primary Schools* (H.M.S.O., 1967) p. 33.
8 Stephen Wiseman, *Education and Environment* (Manchester University Press, Manchester, 1964) p. 167.
9 See the substantial agreement among H. A. Ree, *The Essential Grammar School* (Harrap, London, 1956), F. Stevens, *The Living Tradition* (Hutchinson, London, 1960) and H. A. Davies, *Culture and the Grammar School* (Routledge and Kegan Paul, London, 1965).
10 See R. King, *Values and Involvement in a Grammar School* (Routledge and Kegan Paul, London, 1969) pp. 142–3.
11 Schools' Council: *Inquiry I: Young School Leavers* (H.M.S.O., 1968) p. 233.
12 Ibid., p. 139.
13 J. A. Wankowski, 'G.C.E.s and Degrees' (1969) unpublished research report, University of Birmingham.
14 The classic distinction between democratic, authoritarian and laissez-faire leadership (in youth clubs) was made by Lewin, Lippit and White in 1939. See K. Lewin, R. Lippitt and R. K. White, 'Patterns of Aggressive Behaviour in Experimentally Created "Social Climates"', *Journal of Social Psychology* (1939) vol. 10.
15 Schools' Council: *Inquiry I: Young School Leavers*, pp. 56–8.
16 Ibid., p. 245.
17 W. B. Brookover, 'The Social Roles of Teachers and Pupil Achievement', *American Sociological Review* (1943) vol. 8.
18 For a comprehensive review of research in this area especially at the college level, see W. J. McKeachie, 'Procedures and Techniques of Teaching: A Survey of Experimental Studies' in Nevitt Sanford (ed.), *The American College* (John Wiley, New York, 1964).

> The results of the research on student-centred teaching methods are not impressive [but] ... the possible advantages of student-centred instruction in achieving the goal of application of concepts is supported by the experiments of Bovard, McKeachie, Patton, Carpenter and Davage (pp. 333–4).

19 Elizabeth Monroe Drews and John E. Teahan, 'Parental Attitudes and Academic Achievement', *Journal of Clinical Psychology* (1957) vol. 13. For comment and interpretation of similar research findings see

F. Musgrove, *The Family, Education and Society* (Routledge and Kegan Paul, London, 1966) Ch. 5, 'The Good Home'.
20 R. C. Anderson, 'Learning in Discussion: A résumé of the Authoritarian-Democratic Studies' in W. W. Charters and N. L. Gage (eds.), *Readings in the Social Psychology of Education* (Allyn and Bacon, Boston, 1963).
21 See A. P. Hare, *Social Interaction. An Analysis of Behaviour in Small Groups* (John Wiley, New York, 1959).
22 D. H. Hargreaves, *Social Relations in a Secondary School* (Routledge and Kegan Paul, London, 1967) p. 87.
23 See Stephen Wiseman, op. cit.

> Thus, the chief effect of progressive education appears to be to raise the reading capacity of the children, particularly the backward readers, progressive teachers apparently emphasizing comprehension of language rather than the acquirement of mathematical techniques (p. 107).

24 F. A. Haddon and H. Lytton, 'Teaching Approach and the Development of Divergent Thinking Abilities in Primary Schools', *British Journal of Educational Psychology* (1968) vol. 38. The particular ingredient or aspect of progressive teaching that is effective is always difficult to isolate. Haddon and Lytton suggest that the crucial circumstance is not 'permissiveness' *per se*, but arises from 'the teacher's confidence in the child's ability to think adventurously and in new directions. . . .'
25 Liam Hudson, 'Lieben und Arbeiten' in M. Ash (ed.), *Who are the Progressives Now?* (Routledge and Kegan Paul, London, 1969). Happy children may not be prepared to make the effort that excellence demands. 'The forces that drive a man to be creative have their roots if not in unhappiness, at least in unease. It follows that an education of genuine benevolence may disqualify children from a life of productive thought' (p. 179).
26 A. Etzioni, op. cit., p. 72. Organizations may be high or low in pervasiveness, wide or narrow in scope. Thus a sports club and perhaps a technical college are low in pervasiveness and narrow in scope; a church is high in pervasiveness but narrow in scope; a troopship, prison or asylum is low in pervasiveness but wide in scope; a monastery or boarding school is high in pervasiveness and wide in scope.
27 Erving Goffman, *Asylums* (Anchor Books, Doubleday, New York, 1961) p. 12.

28 *Report of the Royal Commission on the State of Popular Education in England* (the Newcastle Report) 1861.
29 Erving Goffman, op. cit., p. 6.
30 Ibid., p. 4. 'When we review the different institutions in our Western society, we find some that are encompassing to a degree discontinuously greater than the ones next in line.... These establishments I am calling total institutions....'
31 Ibid., p. 189.
32 Ibid., p. 61.
33 See Royston Lambert, Roger Bullock and Spencer Millham, 'The Informal Social System', paper presented to the annual conference of the British Sociological Association, Durham, 1970.
34 J. Wakeford, *The Cloistered Elite* (Macmillan, London, 1969) pp. 44–5, 52 and 91.
35 Royston Lambert, *The Hothouse Society* (Weidenfeld and Nicolson, London, 1968) p. 226.
36 Ibid., p. 364.
37 R. K. Merton, *Social Theory and Social Structure* (The Free Press of Glencoe, Illinois, 1964) pp. 131–94.
38 For a critique of Merton's typology see F. Harary, 'Merton Revisited: A New Classification for Deviant Behaviour', *American Sociological Review* (1966) vol. 31.
39 J. Wakeford, op. cit., p. 134.
40 Talcott Parsons, 'On the Concept of Political Power', *Proceedings of the American Philosophical Society* (1963) vol. 107.
41 E.g. A. Giddens, ' "Power" in the Recent Writings of Talcott Parsons', *Sociology* (1968) vol. 2.
42 A. S. Tannenbaum, 'Control and Effectiveness in a Voluntary Organization', *American Journal of Sociology* (1961–2) vol. 67. Control graphs were constructed. The average height of the curve (or the area under the curve) measured the total power in the organization; the slope of the curve measured its distribution. A negative slope indicated autocratic control, a positive slope democratic control, a flat, low slope laissez-faire control, and a flat high slope polyarchic control.
43 In this further study, democracy in voluntary organizations (but only voluntary organizations) was related to effectiveness as well as morale: see C. G. Smith and A. S. Tannenbaum, 'Organizational Control Structure', *Human Relations* (1963) vol. 16.
44 H. A. Hornstein, D. M. Callahan, E. Fisch and B. A. Benedict, 'Influence and Satisfaction in Organizations', *Sociology of Education* (1968) vol. 41.

CHAPTER THREE

1 As expounded in P. M. Blau, *Exchange and Power in Social Life* (John Wiley, New York, 1964) and G. C. Homans, *Social Behaviour: Its Elementary Forms* (Routledge and Kegan Paul, London, 1961).
2 Percy C. Cohen, *Modern Social Theory* (Heinemann, London, 1968) pp. 121–5.
3 See A. W. Gouldner, 'The Norm of Reciprocity', *American Sociological Review* (1960) vol. 25.
4 Ruth Benedict, *The Chrysanthemum and the Sword* (Routledge and Kegan Paul, London, 1967).
5 Cf. Marc Bloch, *Feudal Society* (translated by L. A. Manyon) (Routledge and Kegan Paul, London, 1961) p. 169.
6 Percy S. Cohen, op. cit., p. 123.
7 Erving Goffman, *Asylums* (Anchor Books, Doubleday, New York, 1961) p. 280.
8 See P. M. Blau, *The Dynamics of Bureaucracy* (University of Chicago Press, Chicago, 1955).
9 L. Cohen, 'Functional Dependence, Exchanges and Power of Influence', *International Journal of Educational Sciences* (1969) vol. 3.
10 John Freeman, *Team Teaching in Britain* (Ward Lock, London, 1969) p. 227.
11 W. O. Hagstrom, *The Scientific Community* (Basic Books, New York, 1965) p. 106.
12 Ibid., p. 111.
13 Ibid., p. 111.
14 Quoted in G. M. Swatez, 'The Social Organization of a University Laboratory', *Minerva* (1970) vol. 8.
15 Cf. E. Jaques, *The Changing Culture of a Factory* (Tavistock Publications, London, 1951) p. 277.
16 C. M. Turner, 'An Organizational Analysis of a Secondary Modern School', *Sociological Review* (1969) vol. 17.
17 Marc Bloch, op. cit.
18 Bertrand de Jouvenal, *Power* (translated by J. F. Huntington) (Hutchinson, London, 1948) p. 302.
19 A. W. Gouldner, *Patterns of Industrial Bureaucracy* (The Free Press, New York, 1954) p. 78.
20 Howard S. Becker, 'The Teacher in the Authority System of the Public School', *Journal of Educational Sociology* (1953–4) vol. 27.

21 C. M. Turner, op. cit.
22 See J. K. Hemphill and A. E. Coons, 'Development of the Leader Behaviour Description Questionnaire' in R. M. Stogdill and A. E. Coons, *Leader Behaviour: Its Description and Measurement* (Ohio State University, 1957).
23 M. Crozier, *The Bureaucratic Phenomenon* (Tavistock Publications, London, 1964) p. 155.
24 See D. L. Keir, *The Constitutional History of Modern Britain 1485–1937* (Black, London, 1943) p. 266.
25 A. W. Gouldner, op. cit., p. 172.
26 J. G. Anderson, 'The Authority Structure of the School: System of Social Exchange', *Educational Administration Quarterly* (1967) vol. 3.
27 F. W. Young, *Initiation Ceremonies: A Cross Cultural Study of Status Dramatization* (Bobbs-Merrill, Indianapolis, 1965).
28 J. W. M. Whiting, R. Kluckhohn and A. Anthony, 'The Function of Male Initiation Ceremonies at Puberty' in E. E. Maccoby, T. M. Newcomb and E. L. Hartley (eds.), *Readings in Social Psychology* (Holt, New York, 1958).
29 See W. J. Ong, 'Latin Language as a Renaissance Puberty Rite', *Studies in Philology* (1959) vol. 56.
30 A. Etzioni, *Complex Organizations* (Free Press of Glencoe, Illinois, 1961) p. 45.
31 Ibid., p. 49.
32 See *The Prince* (translated by N. H. Thomson) (Clarendon Press, London, 1913) Ch. 4.
33 B. Miller, *The Palace School of Muhammad the Conqueror* (Harvard University Press, Cambridge, Mass., 1941) p. 4.
34 Ibid., p. 8.
35 S. M. Dornbusch, 'The Military Academy as an Assimilating Institution', *Social Forces* (1954–5) vol. 33.
36 Royston Lambert, Roger Bullock and Spencer Millham, 'The Informal Social System': a paper presented to the British Sociological Association, University of Durham, 1970.
37 E. Aronson and J. Mills, 'The Effect of Severity of Initiation on Liking for a Group', *Journal of Abnormal and Social Psychology* (1959) vol. 59.
38 L. Festinger, *A Theory of Cognitive Dissonance* (Row, Peterson, Evanston, 1957).
39 Erving Goffman, op. cit., p. 72.

CHAPTER FOUR

1 Gilbert Highet, *The Art of Teaching* (Methuen, University Paperbacks, London, 1963) p. 53.
2 Ibid., p. 53.
3 Cf. John Webb, 'The Sociology of a School', *British Journal of Sociology* (1962) vol. 13. Hostility between staff and pupils is seen as 'the key factor' in boys' secondary modern schools, the teachers' hatred and fatigue leading to aversion. In lower streams especially, teachers may adapt by 'withdrawal' or 'domination'. See David H. Hargreaves, *Social Relations in a Secondary School* (Routledge and Kegan Paul, London, 1967) pp. 103-4.
4 Enid Welsford, *The Fool* (Faber, London, 1965) p. 139.
5 E. Goffman, *Encounters* (Bobbs-Merrill, Indianapolis, 1961).
6 R. A. Stebbins, 'Role Distance, Role Distance Behaviour and Jazz Musicians', *British Journal of Sociology* (1969) vol. 20.
7 See J. Ford, D. Young and S. Box, 'Functional Autonomy, Role Distance and Social Class', *British Journal of Sociology* (1967) vol. 18.
8 Jacob Levine, 'Regression in Primitive Clowning', *Psychoanalytic Quarterly* (1961) vol. 30.
9 J. P. Emerson, 'Negotiating the Serious Import of Humour', *Sociometry* (1969) vol. 32.
10 Ibid.
11 David H. Hargreaves, op. cit., p. 85.
12 Ruth Benedict, *The Chrysanthemum and the Sword* (Routledge and Kegan Paul, London, 1967) p. 111.
13 Ibid., p. 109.
14 Cf. O. E. Klapp, 'Heroes, Villains and Fools as Agents of Social Control', *American Sociological Review* (1954) vol. 19.
15 Cf. P. J. Burke, 'Scapegoating', *Sociometry* (1969) vol. 32.
16 A. Dworkin, 'The Angered: Their Susceptibility to Varieties of Humour', *Journal of Personality and Social Psychology* (1967) vol. 2.
17 Cf. F. Musgrove, *The Family, Education and Society* (Routledge and Kegan Paul, London, 1966) especially Ch. 5; E. M. Drews and J. E. Teahan, 'Parental Attitudes and Academic Achievement', *Journal of Clinical Psychology* (1957) vol. 13; and H. G. Gough, 'What Determines Academic Achievement in High School Students', *Journal of Educational Research* (1953) vol. 46.

18 R. R. Dale, *Mixed or Single-sex School?* (Routledge and Kegan Paul, London, 1969).
19 Ibid., p. 175.
20 Ibid., pp. 184–5.
21 Ibid., p. 63.
22 Ibid., p. 65.
23 Ibid., pp. 178–80.
24 Ibid., p. 237.
25 Ibid., p. 176.
26 G. Tyson, *Some Apparent Effects of Co-education Suggested by a Statistical Investigation of Examination Results* (1928) M.Ed. thesis, Manchester.
27 R. Field, *An Enquiry into the Relative Achievement of Boys and Girls at a First School Certificate Examination in the Six Commoner Subjects of the Curriculum* (1935) M.A. thesis, Birmingham.
28 M. B. Sutherland, 'Co-education and School Attainment', *British Journal of Educational Psychology* (1961) vol. 31.
29 R. R. Dale, 'A Critical Analysis of Research on the Effects of Co-education on Academic Attainment in Grammar Schools', *Educational Research* (1962) vol. 4, and 'An Analysis of Research on Comparative Attainment in Mathematics in Single-sex and Co-educational Maintained Grammar Schools', *Educational Research* (1962) vol. 5.
30 See R. R. Dale, 'Research on Comparative Attainment in English in Single-sex and Co-educational Grammar Schools', *Educational Research* (1964) vol. 6.
31 See Royston Lambert, *The Hothouse Society* (Weidenfeld and Nicolson, London, 1968) p. 354.
32 W. A. L. Blyth, 'The Sociometric Study of Children's Groups in English Schools', *British Journal of Educational Studies* (1960) vol. 8.

CHAPTER FIVE

1 A. Etzioni, *Complex Organizations* (Free Press of Glencoe, Illinois, 1961) pp. 307–8.
2 See Jeremy Bentham, 'Panopticon, or, The Inspection-House', in John Bowring, *The Works of Jeremy Bentham* (Russell and Russell, New York, 1962) vol. 4, pp. 39–66.

3 Quoted by J. Wakeford, *The Cloistered Elite* (Macmillan, London, 1969) pp. 176-7, from K. Kettle, 'Winchester College' in R. E. Gross (ed.), *British Secondary Education, Overview and Appraisal* (Oxford University Press, London, 1965).
4 T. W. Bamford, *The Rise of the Public Schools* (Nelson, London, 1967) p. 61.
5 G. F. Lamb, *The Happiest Days* (Michael Joseph, London, 1959) p. 178.
6 *Children and their Primary Schools*. A report of the Central Advisory Council for Education (England) vol. 1 (H.M.S.O., 1967) p. 395.
7 Basil Bernstein, 'Open Schools, Open Society', *New Society*, 14 September 1967.
8 See F. Musgrove, 'Middle Class Education and Employment in the Nineteenth Century', *Economic History Review* (1961) vol. 14.
9 Ibid. The average figures given are calculated from the data in this paper.
10 See Robin Pedley, *The Comprehensive School* (Penguin Books, Harmondsworth, 1963).
11 See F. Musgrove, op. cit.
12 Cf. B. J. Palisi, 'Some Suggestions about the Transitory-Permanence Dimension of Organizations', *British Journal of Sociology* (1970) vol. 21.
13 P. M. Blau and W. R. Scott, *Formal Organizations* (Routledge and Kegan Paul, London, 1963) p. 227.
14 Reinhard Bendix, *Works and Authority in Industry* (Harper Torchbooks, New York, 1963) p. 214.
15 G. H. Moeller and W. W. Charters, 'Relation of Bureaucratization to Sense of Power among Teachers', *Administrative Science Quarterly* (1966) vol. 10.
16 G. K. Ingham, 'Organizational Size, Orientation to Work and Industrial Behaviour', *Sociology* (1967) vol. 1.
17 See J. K. Hemphill, 'Relationship between the Size of the Group and the Behaviour of Superior Leaders', *Journal of Social Psychology* (1950) vol. 32, and L. F. Carter *et al.*, 'The Relations of Categorizations and Ratings in the Observation of Group Behaviour', *Human Relations* (1951) vol. 4.
18 See L. Cohen, 'The Formal Organization of the School', *Papers in Education* (1969) Anstey College of Education.
19 L. Cohen, *Conceptions of Headteachers Concerning Their Role* (1970) unpublished Ph.D. thesis, Keele.
20 Cf. William Taylor, 'Issues and Problems in Training the School

Administrator' in George Baron and William Taylor, *Educational Administration and the Social Sciences* (Athlone Press, London, 1969) p. 105.
21 M. E. Highfield and A. Pinsent, *A Survey of Rewards and Punishments in Schools* (Newnes Educational Publishing Company, Feltham, Middlesex, 1952) p. 93.
22 Ibid., pp. 82–3.
23 Cf. B. P. Indik, 'Some Effects of Organizational Size on Member Attitudes and Behaviour', *Human Relations* (1963) vol. 16, and 'Organizational Size and Member Participation', *Human Relations* (1965) vol. 18.
24 John H. Goldthorpe, 'Attitudes and Behaviour of Car Assembly Workers: A Deviant Case and a Theoretical Critique', *British Journal of Sociology* (1966) vol. 17.
25 F. Musgrove, *The Family, Education and Society* (Routledge and Kegan Paul, London, 1966) Ch. 6.
26 Robin Pedley, op. cit., pp. 139–40.
27 R. Lynn, 'The Relation Between Educational Achievement and School Size', *British Journal of Sociology* (1959) vol. 10.
28 Peter M. Blau, *Exchange and Power in Social Life* (John Wiley, New York, 1964) p. 323.
29 Ibid., p. 323.

CHAPTER SIX

1 See 'Letters to the Editor', *Guardian*, 5 March 1970.
2 M. Crozier, *The Bureaucratic Phenomenon* (Tavistock Publications, London, 1964) p. 58.
3 Public Schools Commission: Second Report Vol. 1. *Report on Independent Day Schools and Direct Grant Grammar Schools* (H.M.S.O., 1970) para. 299.
4 Ibid., para. 304.
5 A Report of the Central Advisory Council for Education (England): Vol. 1. *Children and their Primary Schools* (H.M.S.O., 1967) para. 1144.
6 Ibid., para. 1142.
7 *Donnison Report*, para. 306.
8 *Plowden Report*, para. 1145.
9 *Donnison Report*, para. 307.

10 *Plowden Report*, para. 1147.
11 *Donnison Report*, para. 313.
12 See W. A. L. Blyth, *English Primary Education* (Routledge and Kegan Paul, London, 1965).
13 See W. B. Davies, 'On the Contribution of Organizational Analysis to the Study of Educational Institutions': paper presented to the British Sociological Association Conference, 1970.
14 See C. L. Sharma, *A Comparative Study of the Processes of Making and Taking Decisions within Schools in the U.K. and U.S.A.* (1963) unpublished Ph.D. thesis, University of London.
15 G. F. Lamb, *The Happiest Days* (Michael Joseph, London, 1959) p. 138.
16 Ibid.
17 See J. Wakeford, *The Cloistered Elite* (Macmillan, London, 1969) pp. 106–7.
18 See Department of Education and Science: *Report of the Study Group on the Government of Colleges of Education* (the 'Weaver Report'), H.M.S.O., 1966. See paras. 109–14 on the Academic Board.

> We regard it as essential that every college should have a properly constituted academic board. We have already recommended that, within the general framework laid down, and in consultation with the appropriate bodies, the board should be responsible for the academic work of the college, for the selection of students and for arrangements for teaching practice (para. 110).
>
> As regards the make-up of the academic board, we think that, in addition to the principal (as chairman) and deputy principal, it should contain those members of the teaching staff who carry the main weight of responsibility in the college, together with reasonable representation of other teaching staff (para. 112).

19 Eric Ashby, *Technology and the Academics* (Macmillan, London, 1963) p. 71.
20 Ibid., p. 101.
21 M. Trow and A. H. Halsey, 'British Academics and the Professorship', *Sociology* (1969) vol. 3.
22 C. M. Turner, 'An Organizational Analysis of a Secondary Modern School', *Sociological Review* (1969) vol. 17.
23 E. Litwak, 'Models of Bureaucracy which Permit Conflict', *American Journal of Sociology* (1961–2) vol. 67.
24 Jacques Barzun has justified the usual American practice of keeping

25 Joan Woodward, 'Management and Technology' in Tom Burns (ed.), *Industrial Man* (Penguin Books, Harmondsworth, 1969).
26 E. Halevy, *England in 1815* (Benn, London, 1949) pp. 535–6.
27 T. W. Bamford, *The Rise of the Public Schools* (Nelson, London, 1967) pp. 74–5.
28 G. F. Lamb, op. cit., p. 81.
29 Royston Lambert, 'The Future of Boarding in Modern Society' in M. Ash (ed.), *Who Are the Progressives Now?* (Routledge and Kegan Paul, London, 1969).
30 G. F. Lamb, op. cit., p. 52.
31 F. D. How, *Six Great Schoolmasters* (Methuen, London, 1905) p. 63.
32 See D. I. Wood, 'What's a Student Council for?' *N.E.A. Journal*, April 1962.
33 See J. A. Chapman, *An Evaluation of the Role of School Councils in Secondary Education* (1969) unpublished M.Sc. dissertation, University of Bradford.
34 Ibid., pp. 239–40.
35 Ibid., p. 230.
36 Ibid., p. 237.
37 Elliott Jaques, *The Changing Culture of a Factory* (Tavistock Publications, London, 1951) pp. 138–55.
38 Ibid., pp. 112–13.
39 Allan Flanders, Ruth Pomeranz and Joan Woodward, *Experiment in Industrial Democracy* (Faber, London, 1958) p. 189.
40 Ibid., p. 186.
41 M. Crozier, op. cit., pp. 204–5.
42 Elliott Jaques, op. cit., p. 279.
43 Cf. T. H. Marshall, 'Reflections on Power', *Sociology* (1969) vol. 3.

Note 24 continued: academics out of university-wide government and confining their self-governing to departmental affairs: the two spheres or levels should be recognized to be distinct and kept distinct. See *The American University: How it Runs, Where it is Going* (Oxford University Press, London, 1969).

CHAPTER SEVEN

1 See Max Weber, *The Theory of Social and Economic Organization*, translated by A. M. Henderson and Talcott Parsons (Oxford University Press, New York, 1947).

2 R. H. Hall, 'The Concept of Bureaucracy: An Empirical Assessment', *American Journal of Sociology* (1963) vol. 69.
3 D. S. Pugh, D. J. Hickson, C. R. Hinings and C. Turner, 'Dimensions of Organization Structure', *Administrative Science Quarterly* (1968) vol. 13.
4 R. C. K. Ensor, *England 1870–1914* (Oxford University Press, London, 1936) p. 114.
5 Ibid., p. 112.
6 Ibid., pp. 10–16.
7 Noel Annan, 'The Intellectual Aristocracy' in J. H. Plumb (ed.), *Studies in Social History* (Longmans, Green, London, 1955).
8 'Competitive Examinations', *Quarterly Review* (1860) vol. 108.
9 *First Report of the Civil Service Inquiry Commission* (1875) p. 27.
10 See F. Musgrove, *The Migratory Elite* (Heinemann, London, 1963) for a general consideration of qualifications and mobility, and R. V. Clements, *Managers: A Study of their Careers in Industry* (Allen & Unwin, London, 1958) pp. 125 and 182, for an examination of formal qualifications and mobility among industrial managers.
11 Joseph Priestley, *Observations Relating to Education* (1788) p. 53.
12 George Chapman, *Treatise on Education* (1790) p. 35.
13 David Williams, *A Treatise on Education* (1774) p. 48.
14 David Williams, *Lectures on Education* (1789) vol. 1, p. 58.
15 Mrs Gaskell, *The Life of Charlotte Bronte*, 3rd edition (1857) vol. 1, p. 199.
16 David Williams, *Lectures on Education*, p. 155.
17 G. F. Lamb, *The Happiest Days* (Michael Joseph, London, 1959) p. 104.
18 Norman Carlisle, *A Concise Description of the Endowed Grammar Schools in England and Wales* (1818) p. 263.
19 T. W. Bamford, *The Rise of the Public Schools* (Nelson, London, 1967) p. 117.
20 Ibid., pp. 117–18.
21 Quoted in Eric Ashby, 'The Academic Profession', *Minerva* (1970) vol. 8.
22 L. S. R. Byrne and E. L. Churchill, *Changing Eton* (Cape, London, 1937) p. 146.
23 Thomas Sheridan, *A Plan of Education for the Young Nobility and Gentry of Great Britain* (1769) p. 74. But cf. William Barrow, *An Essay on Education* (1802) p. 123. Barrow approved of this system because it ensured some individual tuition for the pupil.
24 Vicesimus Knox, *Liberal Education* (1781) vol. 2, pp. 263–4.

25 L. S. R. Byrne and E. L. Churchill, op. cit., p. 148.
26 V. H. H. Green, *The Universities* (Penguin Books, Harmondsworth, 1969) p. 202.
27 H. W. Carless Davis, *A History of Balliol College* (Blackwell, Oxford, 1963) pp. 89–90.
28 Ibid., p. 274.
29 J. B. Morrell, 'Thomas Thomson: Professor of Chemistry and University Reformer', *British Journal for the History of Science* (1969) vol. 4.
30 J. B. Morrell, 'Practical Chemistry in the University of Edinburgh, 1799–1843', *Ambix* (1969) vol. 16.
31 Quoted ibid.
32 See Peter S. Burnham, *The Role of the Deputy Head in Secondary Schools* (1964) University of Leicester, unpublished M.Ed. thesis.
33 Quoted ibid.
34 Quoted ibid.
35 G. Baron, 'Some Aspects of the "Headmaster Tradition"', *Researches and Studies* (1956) no. 14.
36 W. G. Walker, *A History of Oundle School* (Hazell, Watson and Viney Ltd, London, 1956).
37 J. H. Skrine, *A Memory of Edward Thring* (Hazell, Watson and Viney Ltd, London, 1890).
38 W. G. Walker, op. cit.
39 A. I. Tillyard, *A History of University Reform* (1913) p. 352.
40 James M. Wilson, *An Autobiography 1836–1931* (London, 1932).
41 Ibid., p. 80.
42 *Report of the Schools Inquiry Commission* (1868) vol. 1, p. 238.
43 *Report of the Royal Commission on Secondary Education* (1895) vol. 1, p. 209.
44 Ibid., vol. 4, p. 539.
45 One historian has claimed that they commonly earned ten times as much. See T. W. Bamford, op. cit., p. 129. Whilst such differences certainly existed, the average situation was almost certainly less extreme.
46 E.g. Oundle £550, Repton £710, Durham £900, Bedford £1,000, Birmingham £2,000. See *Report of the Schools Inquiry Commission* (1868) vol. 1, p. 238 ff.
47 See Keith Norris, 'What teachers earn', *The Times Educational Supplement*, 13 February 1970, pp. 72–3.
48 T. W. Bamford, 'Public School Town in the Nineteenth Century', *British Journal of Educational Studies* (1957) vol. 6.

49 T. W. Bamford, *The Rise of the Public Schools* (Nelson, London, 1957) p. 132.
50 G. Baron, op. cit.
51 Cf. M. Aiken and J. Hage, 'Organizational Alienation: A Comparative Analysis', *American Sociological Review* (1966) vol. 31.
52 F. Musgrove, 'Experience of Bureaucracy and Attitudes to Industrial Training', *Irish Journal of Education* (1968) vol. 1.
53 G. H. Moeller and W. W. Charters, 'Relation of Bureaucratization to Sense of Power among Teachers', *Administrative Science Quarterly* (1966) vol. 10.

CHAPTER EIGHT

1 G. F. Lamb, *The Happiest Days* (Michael Joseph, London, 1959) p. 122.
2 R. K. Merton, *Social Theory and Social Structure* (The Free Press of Glencoe, Illinois, 1957) p. 218.
3 N. Gross and R. E. Herriott, *Staff Leadership in Public Schools* (Wiley, New York, 1965) pp. 102-3.
4 W. Taylor, 'The Training College Principal', *Sociological Review* (1964) vol. 12.
5 A. J. Toynbee, *Acquaintances* (Oxford University Press, London, 1967) p. 166.
6 Peter M. Blau, *Exchange and Power in Social Life* (Wiley, New York, 1964) p. 319.
7 Cf. H. A. Hornstein et al., 'Influence and Satisfaction in Organizations', *Sociology of Education* (1968) vol. 41.
8 For the distinction between reward power, coercive power, legitimate power, referent power and expert power, see J. R. P. French and B. Raven, 'The Bases of Social Power', in D. Cartwright and A. Zander, *Group Dynamics: Research and Theory* (Tavistock Publications, London, 1960).
9 Quoted in A. Tropp, 'The Changing Status of Teachers in England and Wales', *Year Book of Education* (Evans Bros., London, 1953).
10 W. Taylor, op. cit.
11 P. Collison and J. Millen, 'University Chancellors, Vice-Chancellors and College Principals: A Social Profile', *Sociology* (1969) vol. 3.

12 See A. W. Gouldner, *Patterns of Industrial Bureaucracy* (Free Press, New York, 1954).
13 L. Cohen, *Conceptions of Headteachers Concerning Their Role* (1970) unpublished Ph.D. thesis, Keele.
14 M. Crozier, *The Bureaucratic Phenomenon* (Tavistock Publications, London, 1964) p. 155.
15 F. J. Roethlisberger and W. J. Dickson, *Management and the Worker* (Harvard University Press, Cambridge, Mass., 1939) p. 575.
16 B. F. Rice, 'Sam's School', *Times Educational Supplement* (6 March 1970) p. 4.
17 E.g. A. J. M. Sykes, 'Economic Interest and the Hawthorne Researches', *Human Relations* (1965) vol. 18.
18 Alex Carey, 'The Hawthorne Studies: A Radical Criticism', *American Sociological Review* (1967) vol. 32.
19 J. H. Goldthorpe, 'Attitudes and Behaviour of Car Assembly Workers: A Deviant Case and A Theoretical Critique', *British Journal of Sociology* (1966) vol. 17.
20 N. Gross and R. E. Herriott, op. cit.
21 Ibid., p. 104.
22 Ibid., p. 151.
23 F. E. Fiedler, 'A Note on Leadership Theory: The Effect of Social Barriers between Leaders and Followers', *Sociometry* (1957) vol. 20.
24 L. Cohen, op. cit.
25 F. E. Fiedler, 'The Leader's Psychological Distance and Group Effectiveness' in D. Cartwright and A. Zander, *Group Dynamics: Research and Theory* (Tavistock Publications, London, 1960).
26 Chris Argyris, *Executive Leadership* (Harper and Bros., New York, (1953) p. 105.
27 E. E. Jones, K. G. Gergen and R. G. Jones, 'Tactics of Ingratiation among Leaders and Subordinates in a Status Hierarchy', *Pyschological Monographs* (1963) no. 77.
28 See F. E. Fiedler, *Leader Attitudes and Group Effectiveness* (University of Illinois Press, Urbana, Illinois, 1958). Cf. C. M. Turner, 'An Organizational Analysis of a Secondary Modern School', *Sociological Review* (1969) vol. 17:

> What contact they [the staff] had with the Headmaster always contained lavish praise for their work, but this was felt not to be based on accurate knowledge and was therefore not acceptable in terms of social exchange. Furthermore it was subject to the law of diminishing marginal returns. The less praise is given, the more it is valued.

29 G. C. Homans, *Social Behaviour. Its Elementary Forms* (Routledge and Kegan Paul, London, 1961) p. 306.
30 Ibid., p. 312. Cf. Peter M. Blau, op. cit., p. 134.
31 Peter S. Burnham, 'The Deputy Head' in Bryan Allen (ed.), *Headteachers for the Seventies* (Basil Blackwell, Oxford, 1968).
32 W. Taylor, 'The Training College Principal', *Sociological Review* (1964) vol. 12.
33 L. Cohen, op. cit.
34 Peter S. Burnham, 'The Deputy Head', op. cit.
35 Ibid.

CHAPTER NINE

1 See J. D. Thompson and W. J. McEwen, 'Organizational Goals and Environment', *American Sociological Review* (1958) vol. 23.
2 See F. Musgrove and P. H. Taylor, *Society and the Teacher's Role* (Routledge and Kegan Paul, London, 1969) Ch. 3, 'The Expectations of Parents'.
3 See Rowland Eustace, 'The Origins of Self-Government of University Staffs': a paper presented at the annual conference of the British Sociological Association, Durham, 1970. Although the formal power of graduates is often considerable, it has been little exercised since the First World War except at Oxford and London. London University graduates sought a voice in university government

> on the possibly rather special plea that this would make London appear more like a university. At all events, they were granted this request by the Act of 1858, which gave no representation to staff. They become a major and immensely disruptive force in the government of the old university, and a very considerable one under the constitution of 1900–30, when staff did have representation. Their position remains, today, sufficient for instance to have delayed amendments to the composition of the London Senate that it may be surmised would otherwise have followed the Saunders Report of 1966.

4 Elton Mayo, *The Social Problems of an Industrial Civilization* (Routledge and Kegan Paul, London, 1949) p. 98.
5 Ibid., Ch. 2: 'The Rabble Hypothesis and Its Corollary, the State Absolute'.

6 There are now many discussions of these contrasted approaches to the study of organizations; see, for example, David Silverman, 'Formal Organizations or Industrial Sociology: Towards a Social Action Analysis of Organizations', *Sociology* (1968) vol. 2, and Martin Albrow, 'The Study of Organizations – Objectivity or Bias?' in Julius Gould (ed.), *Penguin Social Sciences Survey 1968* (Penguin Books, Harmondsworth, 1968).

7 See M. Crozier, *The Bureaucratic Phenomenon* (Tavistock Publications, London, 1964).

8 John Wakeford, *The Cloistered Elite* (Macmillan, London, 1969) p. 177.

9 See F. Musgrove and A. G. Smithers, 'Attitudes to Industrial Training of Engineering Students on Sandwich Courses', *International Journal of Educational Sciences* (1969) vol. 3, and F. Musgrove (ed.), *Sandwich Course Studies* (University of Bradford, 1970).

10 See D. Child and F. Musgrove, 'Career Orientations of University Freshmen', *Educational Review* (1969) vol. 21.

11 Marie Jahoda, *The Education of Technologists* (Tavistock Publications, London, 1963) p. 202.

12 Ibid., pp. 202–3.

13 Martin Trow, 'Problems for Polytechnics: An American Point of View', *Universities Quarterly* (1969) vol. 23.

14 W. A. L. Blyth, *English Primary Education* (Routledge and Kegan Paul, London, 1965) vol. 2, p. 79.

15 Ibid., vol. 1, pp. 20–1.

16 Cf. C. M. Turner, 'An Organizational Analysis of a Secondary Modern School', *Sociological Review* (1969) vol. 17:

> Under the various Nuffield Projects, C.S.E. Panels and Development Centres, the teacher gives up this independence (as sole arbiter of what is taught in his classroom and how it is taught) in return for a part in planning a more rational system in large-scale units.... As the teacher loses his independence, so too does the school.

See also W. B. Davies, 'On the Contribution of Organizational Analysis to the Study of Educational Institutions', a paper presented at the annual conference of the British Sociological Association, Durham, 1970.

17 Ronald G. Corwin, *A Sociology of Education* (Appleton-Century-Crofts, New York, 1965) p. 39.

18 See Asher Tropp, 'The Changing Status of Teachers in England and Wales', *Year Book of Education* (Evans Bros., London, 1953).

19 Vicars Bell, *The Dodo* (Faber, London, 1950) p. 96.
20 See George Baron, 'Some Aspects of the "Headmaster Tradition"', *Researches in Education* (1956) no. 14.
21 Ibid.
22 Whether there has been a 'disproportionate' growth of internal bureaucracy is very doubtful. As compared to expenditure on academic salaries, expenditure on administrative salaries in universities has actually fallen progressively between 1949 and 1965 – from 13·0 per cent to 10·6 per cent.
    See Michael Shattock, 'A Changing Pattern of University Administration', *Universities Quarterly* (1970) vol. 24.
23 E. P. Thompson, 'The Business University', *New Society*, 19 February 1970. Thompson's celebrated attack is against the Vice-Chancellor, and the Council as his compliant tool. The Council does not appear to have taken any initiative in the conduct that Thompson criticizes. But the composition of Council is seen as ominous – out of nine co-opted lay members, eight are leading industrialists.
24 For an interesting comment on the role of rumour in academic policy-making in a polytechnic, see David W. Jary, 'General and Vocational Courses in Polytechnics', *Universities Quarterly* (1969) vol. 24.
25 Cf. Peter Blau, *Bureaucracy in Modern Society* (Random House, New York, 1956). Ritualism, over-conformity and resistance to change often arise from status-anxieties and consequent feelings of insecurity. 'Rigid adherence to the established routine is a defense mechanism against feelings of insecurity' (p. 90).
26 Rowland Eustace, 'The Origins of Self-Government of University Staffs'.
27 Ibid.
28 Rowland Eustace, 'The Government of Scholars' in David Martin (ed.), *Anarchy and Culture* (Routledge and Kegan Paul, London, 1969).
29 Ibid.
30 See Alan Dawe, 'The Two Sociologies', *British Journal of Sociology* (1970) vol. 21. 'There are, then, two sociologies: a sociology of social system and a sociology of social action.' For the latter: 'Society is thus the creation of its members; the product of their construction of meaning, and of the action and relationships through which they attempt to impose that meaning on their historical situations.'
31 For a lucid account of these issues, see Percy S. Cohen, *Modern Social Theory* (Methuen, London, 1969) pp. 69–94.

32 See John H. Goldthorpe, David Lockwood, Frank Bechhofer and Jennifer Platt, *The Affluent Worker: Industrial Attitudes and Behaviour* (Cambridge University Press, London, 1969).

33 See John H. Goldthorpe, 'Attitudes and Behaviour of Car Assembly Workers: A Deviant Case and a Theoretical Critique', *British Journal of Sociology* (1966) vol. 17.

34 See Martin Trow and A. H. Halsey, 'British Academics and the Professorship', *Sociology* (1969) vol. 3.

35 Jacques Barzun, *The House of Intellect* (Secker and Warburg, London, 1959) pp. 122–3.

36 Burton R. Clark, *The Open Door College* (McGraw-Hill, New York, 1960) p. 149.

37 Ibid, p. 152.

38 See W. G. Walker, *A History of Oundle School* (Hazell, Watson and Viney Ltd, London, 1956).

39 See R. K. Merton, *Social Theory and Social Structure* (The Free Press of Glencoe, Illinois, 1957) pp. 387–420. For a study of citizens' attitudes to a new English university conducted in these terms see F. Musgrove and T. Derrick, 'Attitudes to a New University: The Expectations of Locals and Cosmopolitans', *Research in Education* (1969) no. 2.

40 E.g. P. M. Blau and W. R. Scott, *Formal Organizations: A Comparative Approach* (Routledge and Kegan Paul, London, 1963) pp. 60–74.

41 E.g. S. Box and S. Cotgrove, 'The Productivity of Scientists in Industrial Research Laboratories', *Sociology* (1968) vol. 2. For studies of university students' local-cosmopolitan orientations see D. Child and F. Musgrove, op. cit., and S. Box and J. Ford, 'Commitment to Science: A Solution to Student Marginality?', *Sociology* (1967) vol. 1.

42 See Tom Burns and G. M. Stalker, *The Management of Innovation* (Tavistock Publications, London, 1961) Ch. 9, and M. Dalton, 'Conflicts Between Staff and Line Managers' in T. Burns (ed.), *Industrial Man* (Penguin Books, Harmondsworth, 1969) pp. 265–80.

43 See B. G. Glaser, 'The Local–Cosmopolitan Scientist', *American Journal of Sociology* (1963) vol. 69; L. C. Goldberg and A. H. Rubenstein, 'Local–Cosmopolitan: Unidimensional or Multidimensional?', *American Journal of Sociology* (1965) vol. 70, and S. Box and S. Cotgrove, 'Scientific Identity, Occupational Selection, and Role Strain', *British Journal of Sociology* (1966) vol. 17.

44 D. J. De Solla Price, *Little Science, Big Science* (Columbia University Press, New York, 1963) p. 85.

45 Theodore Caplow and Reece J. McGee, *The Academic Market-place* (Anchor Books, Doubleday, New York, 1965) p. 71.
46 Ibid., p. 177.
47 Martin Trow and A. H. Halsey, op. cit.
48 A. W. Gouldner, 'Cosmopolitans and Locals: II. Toward an Analysis of Latent Social Roles', *Administrative Science Quarterly* (1957–8) vol. 2.
49 See David Riesman, *Constraint and Variety in American Education* (Anchor Books, Doubleday, New York, 1965).
50 John Wakeford, *The Cloistered Elite* (Macmillan, London, 1969) pp. 162–72.
51 J. Kob, 'Definition of the Teacher's Role' in A. H. Halsey, Jean Floud and C. Arnold Anderson, *Education, Economy and Society* (The Free Press of Glencoe, Illinois, 1961).
52 W. G. Bennis et al., 'Reference Groups and Loyalties in the Out-Patient Department', *Administrative Science Quarterly* (1958) vol. 2, pp. 481–500.
53 D. M. Toomey, 'Local–Cosmopolitan Differences Amongst Teachers Taking Higher Degrees', *Educational Review* (1970) vol. 22.
54 M. Crozier, op. cit., p. 85.
55 E.g. C. E. Bidwell, 'The School as a Formal Organization' in J. G. Marsh (ed.), *Handbook of Social Organization* (Rand McNally, Chicago, 1965) p. 992.
56 E.g. Neal Gross et al., *Explorations in Role Analysis* (John Wiley, New York, 1958) p. 100.
57 J. D. Grambs, *Schools, Scholars and Society* (Prentice-Hall, New Jersey, 1965) p. 159.
58 A. Ponsonby, *The Decline of the Aristocracy* (Fisher Unwin, 1912) pp. 207–8.
59 Ibid., pp. 213 and 219.
60 Ibid., p. 209.
61 *Children and their Primary Schools:* A report of the Central Advisory Council for Education (England) 1967, vol. 1, p. 189. Most commentators see the timed and unseen written examinations as the cause of standardization (though it is more properly seen as a symptom): e.g. Gilbert Highet, *The Art of Teaching* (Methuen, London, 1963): 'A room full of candidates for a big examination, resembles nothing so much as an assembly-line at the Ford Works' (p. 118).
62 See J. K. Galbraith, *The New Industrial State* (Penguin Books, Harmondsworth, 1969) p. 43.
63 J. Woodward, *Management and Technology* (H.M.S.O., 1958).

64 Tom Burns and G. M. Stalker, *The Management of Innovation* (Tavistock Publications, London, 1961) p. 83.
65 Ibid., p. 120.
66 Ibid., pp. 120-1.
67 J. E. Hebden, M. J. Rose and W. H. Scott, 'Management Structure and Computerization', *Sociology* (1969) vol. 3.
68 M. Crozier, op. cit., p. 158.
69 Ibid., p. 158.

CHAPTER TEN

1 Liam Hudson, *Contrary Imaginations* (Methuen, London, 1966) p. 114.
2 Cf. F. Musgrove, 'Curriculum Objectives', *Journal of Curriculum Studies* (1968) vol. 1.
3 Cf. James S. Coleman, 'Education in the Age of Computers and Mass Communication', *Hopkins-Brookings Lecture Series* (Johns Hopkins Press, Baltimore, 1970).
4 Michael Huberman, 'Democratization of Secondary and Higher Education', *Times Educational Supplement*, 21 August 1970, pp. 10 and 27.
5 Richard Neville, *Play Power* (Jonathan Cape, London, 1970) p. 278.
6 See Theodore Roszak, *The Making of a Counter Culture* (Faber, London, 1970).
7 E.g. Robert Theobald, *The Challenge of Abundance* (Mentor Books, New York, 1962). Theobald is an advocate of a Guaranteed Annual Income for all Americans, made necessary and possible by automation and the consequent leisure and abundance.
8 G. K. Galbraith, *The New Industrial State* (Penguin Books, Harmondsworth, 1969) p. 365.
9 Ibid., pp. 366-7. Cf. William H. Whyte, *The Organization Man* (Penguin Books, Harmondsworth, 1960) p. 136. 'Common to these men [executives] is an average work week that runs between fifty and sixty hours.'
10 Herbert Marcuse, *Eros and Civilization* (Sphere Books, London, 1969). 'Within the total structure of the repressed personality, surplus-repression is that portion which is the result of specific societal conditions sustained in the specific interest of domination' (p. 81).
11 Ibid., p. 84.

12 Herbert Marcuse, *One Dimensional Man* (Sphere Books, London, 1968) p. 23.
13 C. P. Snow, 'The Corridors of Power', *The Listener*, 18 April 1957.
14 G. K. Galbraith, op. cit., p. 371.
15 Ruth Benedict, *Patterns of Culture* (Routledge and Kegan Paul, London, 1961) pp. 199–200.
16 Bertrand Russell, *Power* (Basic Books, New York, 1940) p. 12.
17 C. Argyris, *Executive Leadership* (Harper and Bros., New York, 1953) p. 81.

Index

Abbotsholme, 82, 83
academic self-government, 129
achievement
 academic, 65
 concept of, 17–18
'action approach'
 to organization studies, 130
 to power and authority, 4
adaptation of schoolboys, 22–3, 24
administrative staff, 61–2
A-level results, 18, 65–6
alienation, 41–2, 43, 61, 64, 104
Alvarez, L., 33–4
ambition, 137–8
American Coast Guard Corps, 42–3
American schools, see under schools
Annan, N., 91
anxiety, 117, 143
Argyris, C., 117, 151
army, the, 45, 90
Arnold, Matthew, 4, 75, 94, 103, 108, 109
Aronson, E., and Mills, J., 43–4
Art of Teaching, The, 46–7
Ashby, E., 9, 76–7
assistant masters, 75–6, 88, 98, 101
Assistant Masters' Association, 103
Atkinson, F. G., 133
attainment
 in American universities, 15
 of goals, 13–15
 in primary schools, 15–16
 in secondary modern schools, 21
authority, aspects of, 1–5, 30
autonomy
 and architecture, 56, 58
 of the main curriculum, 12
 of primary schools, 73, 124–5
 of public schools, 125
 of schoolboys, 80–1

Barclay, J., 92
Baron, G., 128
Barzun, J., 131
Beacon Hill, 82–3
Becker, H. S., 35–6
Bedales, 82
Bell, Vicars, 127
Benedict, R., 49–50, 151
Bentham, Jeremy, 55–6, 126
Bernstein, B., 58
Bill of Rights (1689), 37, 91
Blau, P. M., 31, 61, 66
Bloch, M., 35
Blyth, W. A. L., 73, 124–5
Board of Education, 127, 128, 140
boarding schools, see under schools
boundaries, concept of, 6, 7, 58
Brontë, Charlotte, 92
Brookover, W. B., 19
Brunel University, 123
Bryce Commission, 59
bureaucracy
 'ideal-type', 88–9
 historical development of, 90–1
bureaucratization
 of army, 190
 of civil service, 90–1
 of education, 91–103, 126–8
 and power, 104–5
 and size of administration, 61–2

Burnham Committee, 163
Burns T., and Stalker, G. M., 142
Butler, Henry Montague, 102, 103
Butler, Samuel, 107

Cambridge University
  alumni as pressure group, 121
  development of mathematics at, 11–12
  growth of in nineteenth century, 101
  tutorial system at, 94, 95–6
Caplow, T., and McGee, R. J., 134
Carlisle, N., 94
centralization, 89–90, 126–7
Certificate of Secondary Education, 125
Chapman, George, 92
Children in their Primary Schools, see Plowden Report
civil service, the, 7–8, 91, 108–9
Clarendon Commission (1864), 59, 60, 75, 93, 99, 102, 127
Clark, B., 132
classes, size of, 55
classics, 11
Clifton, 101
co-educational schools, *see under* schools
coercion, 41–2, 43
'cognitive dissonance', 44
Cohen, L., 31–2, 62, 119
colleges of advanced technology, 9, 61, 125
colleges of education, 76, 125
Committee of Council for Education, 126
communication, 68–87
Companies Act (1862), 90
comprehensive schools, *see under* schools
compulsory games, 139–40
conflict, 5, 68–9, 77
conformity, 25
Constitutional Code, The, 126
consultation, in schools, 73–4, 75, 78
control, 55, 81
co-operation, 34
corporal punishment, 63
Corwin, R. G., 126
'cosmopolitans', 133–8, 143–4
counter-culture, the, 147–8
court jesters, 47–8
creativity, 19
Crozier, M., 36–7, 71, 85–6, 112, 122, 138, 141, 145

curricula
  collection, 6
  formal, 11–12
  integrated, 6, 7, 10
curricular 'relevance', 39, 41
curricular values, 8
Curry, W. B., 82
Curzon, Lord, 121
cyberculture, 146, 148

Dahrendorf, R., 3, 4, 5
Dale, R. R., 50–1, 53–4
Dartington Hall, 82
Day Training Colleges, 22
decision-making, in schools, 73–5, 77–80
defensiveness, 50
deputy heads, 118–19. *See also* ushers
deviance, typologies of, 24–5
'difficult children', 64
Digest of Schools and Charities, 59
Diploma of Technology, 123
Directors of Education, 112, 128
discipline, 14, 43, 51, 74
'dominant social groups', 8
Donnison Report, 70, 71–3, 125
Dornbusch, S. M., 42–3
Douglas, J. W. B., 15

eccentricity, 6
efficiency, 68, 69, 90
eleven-plus examination, 125
Endowed Schools Act (1869), 91, 100
Endowed Schools (Masters) Act (1908), 103
Eros and Civilization, 149
Eton
  'Dog Kennel', 57
  Hawtrey's mathematics department, 11, 94
  headmaster's income, 93, 98
  recommendations of Clarendon Commission, 75
  salaries of assistant masters, 102
  schoolboy rebellion, 80
  terms of employment, 95
  tutorial system, 94
  under-master, 99
Etzioni, A., 21, 41, 43
Eustace, R., 129
examinations
  A-level, 18, 65–6

authorizing subjects, 19, 21
development of system of, 91
external, 125
O-level, 16, 65-6
open-book, 140
and pupil–teacher relationship, 32
results in, in co-educational schools, 52-3
exchange theory, *see* social exchange, theory of
expressive demands, 64-5
extra-curriculum, 11-12

Factory Act (1833), 126
Felsted School, 59, 99
Festinger, L., 44
Fiedler, F. E., 116
Field, R., 52
financial control, in schools, 71-2, 80
Forster's Education Act (1870), 30
foundation masters, 93-4, 99
Fremlington Endowed School, 99
Fry, T. C., 100

Galbraith, J. K., 142, 149-50
gifts, in education, 30-45
Glacier Metal Company, 69, 84-5, 86
goals
 acceptance and rejection of, 24
 attainment of, 13, 14-15, 117
 educational, 146-7
 of grammar schools, 16-17
 instrumental, 64, 65
 organizational, 9-11
Goffman, E., 21-4, 31, 44, 48
Goldthorpe, J. H., 64
Gouldner, A. W., 35, 38, 135
Governess, The, 92
governesses, 92-3
Grambs, J. D., 139
grammar schools, *see under* schools
Grantham School, 103
Gross, N., and Herriott, R. E., 114-15
'group cohesiveness', 20

Halsey, A. H., 77, 130
Handbook of Suggestions for the Consideration of Teachers, 140
Hargreaves, D. H., 20-1, 49

Harrow
 establishment of lower school, 99
 salaries of assistant masters, 102
 schoolboy rebellion, 80-1
 'Turret Room', 57
Hawthorne Studies, 112-14, 121
Hawtrey, Stephen, 11, 81, 94
Hayman, Henry, 101-2
headmasters
 American, 108
 attitudes of to parents, 119
 authoritarian, 60
 bureaucratic, 107-8
 Commissions on, 75
 conceptions of role, 116
 democratic, 60
 despotic, 47, 70
 Donnison Report on, 73
 effective, 111
 and external communications, 118
 goals of, 10, 106
 good, 106-19
 income of in nineteenth century, 102-3
 innovatory, 111-12
 of large schools, 62-3, 67
 legitimating characteristics of, 109-11
 of maintained schools, 71
 nineteenth-century, 108
 paths of promotion for, 106-7
 power of, 6, 29, 36, 59, 60, 68, 70, 72, 98, 109
 pre-bureaucratic, 93-4, 107
 of primary schools, 73
 and promotion, 31
 as protectors, 35-6
 of public schools, 93-4, 109
 relationship of
  with deputy, 118
  with staff, 113-15
 of secondary schools, 73
 of secondary modern schools, 110
 sub-professional status of, 70
 succession problems of, 111
 teaching, 107
Head Masters' Association, 127
Head Masters' Conference, 127
H.M.I.s, 110, 126-7, 128
hierarchical systems of organization, 89-91
high achievers, 19-20
Highet, G., 46-7

hippies, 40, 43
Holmes–Morant circular, 110
Homans, G. C., 117, 118
Hope, Thomas Charles, 97
Huberman, M., 147
Hudson, L., 21, 146
'human relations school', 115–16, 121
humanities, the, 8, 9, 18–19
humour, and power, 46–50

initiation, 40–1, 43–4
'input', 120, 130, 131
instrumental demands, 64–5
'investment' in education, 38–9

Jacques, E., 3, 84, 86
Jahoda, M., 123–4
James, John, 93
Japanese culture, 30, 49–50
jazz musicians, 48
jester-pupils, 49
Jex-Blake, T. W., 102
John Lewis Partnership, 69, 85
Joint Matriculation Board, 52
De Jouvenal, B., 35

Kansas City High School, 83–4
Kay-Shuttleworth, Sir James, 126, 127
Keate, J., 150
Keighley Grammar School, 83–4
Kennedy, B. H., 103
King, R., 16–17
knowledge
  high status, 7
  selection and organization of, 6
  stratification of, 7, 8, 9
Knox, Vicesimus, 95
Kob, J., 136–7

Lambert, R., 23–4, 43
Lane, Homer, 82
leadership, effective, 114 ff.
leadership styles, 62
League of Women Voters, 26
Leicestershire Plan, 112
Leighton Park, 82
liberal studies, 9, 19
licensing, 37
'Little Commonwealth', the, 82
Litwak, E., 78
local education authorities, 72, 74, 79

'locals', 133–8, 143
Lockwood, D., 130
low achievers, 19
Lowe, Robert, 127
loyalty, studies of, 134–5
Lumley Secondary Modern School, 20, 49
Lynn, R., 65–6

Machiavelli, Niccolo, 42
Maine, Sir Henry, 94
Mannheim, K., 8
Mansfield Grammar School, 94
Marcuse, H., 146, 149
Marlborough, 57
Master of Education, Degree of, 109
mathematics, 11, 19, 94
Mayo, E., 69, 113, 121–2, 147
'mechanisms of segregation', 78
Merton, R. K., 24, 133
Moberly, George, 81, 139
morale, 20, 26, 64, 114
morning assemblies, 68, 113
motivation, 64

National Foundation for Educational Research, 63
Neill, A. S., 82
Newcastle Commission (1860), 22, 110
'normative structure', 14
normative totality, 23
Northcote–Trevelyan Report, 91
Nottingham High School, 59

Old Boys, 6, 121
O-level results, 16, 65–6
open-door colleges, 132–3
open-planning, 55–7, 58
Organization Man, The, 105
organization studies, 89, 121 f., 130, 133–4, 142–3
organizational and personality dimensions in education, 144
Oundle, 93, 98, 100–1, 133
'output', 120, 138, 141, 142
over-achievement, 17–18
Oxbridge, 7–8
Oxford and Cambridge 'Locals', 91

Palace School of the Grand Seraglio, 42
'panopticon', 56
parental attitudes, 15, 16

parents
  authoritarian, 20
  and decision-taking, 19–20
  as pressure groups, 120
Parent–Teacher Associations, 6
Parsons, T., 3, 9, 25–6
participation, 68–87
'payment-by-results', 127, 140
Pedley, R., 65
personal interconnectedness, 7–8
'pervasiveness', 21
Peters, R. S., 2
Playfair Commission, 91
'plebiscitarianism', 86
Plowden Report, 15–16, 58, 70, 71–2, 141
polytechnics, 125, 129
Ponsonby, Arthur, 139–40
Poor Law, 126
power
  authoritarian, 19
  and authority, 1–2, 3
  and bureaucratization, 104
  as a circulating medium, 25–6, 66
  coercive, 4
  and decision-making, 19
  definition of, 9
  democratic, 19
  distribution of, 70
  English academics' attitudes to, 135
  environment, the, 120–45
  'expert-', 110
  of headmasters, *see under* headmasters
  and innovation, 112
  of the modern state, 35
  normative, 14
  organizational, 25–8
  personal, 3, 4
  and production, 142
  of professors, 77
  remunerative, 14
  and responsibility, 86
  of schools, *see under* schools
  and social imbalance, 31
  struggles, 5
  suspended, 36–8
  of teachers, *see under* teachers
  as zero-sum phenomenon, 25, 26, 98
power structure
  of feudal Europe, 35
  of schools, 30–1

  of society, 9
pressure groups, 120–1
Preston, John, 96
'price', concept of, 39–40, 43
primary schools, *see under* schools
'proactive status', 44
productivity, 19, 20, 114
professional courses, 39
professors, 96–8
'progressiveness', 20
promotion, 31, 89, 90, 111
protection, 35–6
Public Schools Act (1868), 91, 100
public schools, *see under* schools *and* individual school entries
punishment, 86–7
pupil-centred teaching, 19, 21
pupil power, experiments in, 81–2
pupil teachers, 31
pupils
  abilities of, 15
  as clients, 5, 69
  and decision-making, 19
  exchange relationship of with teachers, 32
  grammar school, 65
  L.E.A. boarding school, 23–4
  as 'lower-order' participants, 69
  as 'patients', 5, 69
  as 'products', 69
  public school, 23–5
  rights of, 131, 132
  secondary modern, 21, 65
  as 'self-employed', 69

Quarterly Review, 98
Queen Mary's Grammar School, Walsall, 59

reading ability, 21
rebellion, 24
recruitment, 4, 13–14, 135–6, 152
Reddie, Cecil, 82
Regulations for Secondary Schools, The, 128
relationships, 20–1
religious instruction, 19
residential principle, the, 21–2
resolution, 50
responsibility and power, 86
retreatism, 24

Revised Code (1862), 127, 140
Riesman, D., 136
rights, 4, 131
rigour, 43
Robbins Report, 125, 129
role distance behaviour, 48
role obligations, of schoolboys, 48
Royal Commission on Public Schools, 95, 98
Royal Commission on Secondary Education, 103
Royal Society, the, 105
'rudeness', 49
Rugby
  Arnold as headmaster, 108, 109
  Clarendon Commission on, 75
  establishment of lower school, 99–100
  power struggles at, 121
  salaries of assistant masters, 102, 103
  schoolboy rebellion, 80–1

Sanderson, F. W., 100
sandwich courses, 104, 122–3, 124, 125
sarcasm, as form of control, 47
scapegoat, jester as, 50
schoolboy rebellions, 80–1
school conditions, 16
school councils, 48, 69–70, 80, 81–4
school leaving age, 38
school managers, 127
school rules, 37–8
schools
  American, 19, 35–6, 41, 62, 81, 83
  boarding, 23, 43, 68, 83
  bureaucratization of, 91–103, 126–8
  co-educational, 50–2
  comprehensive, 71, 74
  day, 68
  direct-grant, 18, 61, 71
  eighteenth-century, 80–1
  elementary, 30, 59, 126, 140
  endowed grammar, 59, 60, 91, 94
  of the future, 149–50
  grammar, 16–17, 59, 74, 83, 122
  impotent, 13–28
  independent, 18, 61
  and industrial organizations, 3, 5, 34, 65
  large, 62–7
  maintained secondary, 59–60, 128
  nineteenth-century, 91–2, 93–4, 99–103
  non-selective, 18
  over-potent, 17, 18
  'pervasive', 21
  potent, 15, 18
  power of over pupils, 29
  power relations in, 6
  power structure of, 30–1
  preparatory, 59
  primary, 15–16, 21, 73, 74, 120, 122, 124–5
  progressive, 40–1
  public, 11, 23–4, 59, 80–1, 91, 98–100, 121, 122, 140
  ragged, 30
  relationship of to environment, *throughout, but see esp.*, 4–6, 9 ff. 70, 120 ff., 141–2, 152
  retroactive power of, 44
  scope of, 21
  shape of, 55–9
  sixteenth-century, 40–1
  size of, 59–67
  Sunday, 30
  'totalization' of power in, 27–8
  welfare functions of, 109
Schools Council, the, 7
science, 11, 19
scientists
  compared with teachers, 33–4
  status of, 8
'scope', 21
Scott, A. E., 102
Scott, W. R., 61
secondary modern schools, *see under* schools
selection, 23, 132
sex, 51–5
Shakespeare, William, 48
Sharma, C. L., 73–4
Sherborne, 60
Sheridan, Thomas, 95
Shils, E., 7, 8
Shrewsbury, 60, 103
sixth form, 65
Snow, C. P., 150
social distance, 116, 117, 118
social environment
  relation of schools to, *see under* schools
  and curricula, 7, 12

social exchange, theory of, 29–37, 44
social function, 10
social science, 9
social taboos, 48–9
staff
  administrative, 61–2
  appointment of, 70, 72
  loyalty, 138
  meetings, 75, 76
  time off for, 72
standardization, 126, 138–45
status
  and approval, 117
  conferred by endurance, 44
  conferring protection, 115–16
  and distribution of information, 79
  of educational institutions, 12
  and freedom to take time off, 72
  of headmasters, 70
'student power', 80
subjects
  authoritativeness of, 18–19
  as bureaucracies, 7
  as centres of power, 6–7
Suleiman the Magnificent, 42
Summerhill, 82
superior–subordinate relationships, 117
Sutherland, M. B., 53

Tannenbaum, A. S., 26
Taunton Commission (1868), 59, 60, 75, 99, 102, 127
Taylor, W., 108
teacher-centred teaching, 19, 21
teachers
  ambitious, 137–8
  attitudes and satisfactions of, 104
  as authorities, 2
  authoritarian, 20, 31–2
  autocratic, 18
  'cosmopolitan', 136
  and decision making, 13–14, 18–19, 20, 21
  democratic, 18
  laissez-faire, 18
  power of, 3, 5, 6, 13–14, 18–19, 20, 21
  relationship of with employer, 69
  relationships of with colleagues, 31, 32–3, 78
  restrictions on, 63–4
  status of, 58

teaching methods, 20–1, 140
team teaching, 33, 107
technical colleges, 11, 120, 122–4
technology, 11, 149
Temple, Frederick, 101
tension, 117
Test Acts, 37
Theobald, R., 148
Thring, E., 76, 100
Tonbridge School, 95
Toomey, D. M., 137
'Tory Dozen', the, 31
'total institution', 13, 21–3
totality, concept of, 23
Toynbee, A. J., 108
training 10–11
training college principals, 108, 110, 118
Treatise on Education, 92
Trow, M., 77, 123–4, 130
Turner, C. M., 34, 36
tutorial systems, 94, 95–6
tutors, private, 92
Tyson, G., 52

unhappiness, 117
universities
  American, 15, 43–4
  'comprehensive', 132
  de-bureaucratization of, 128–9
  development of, in nineteenth century, 94–6
  government of, 76–7
  new technological, 8–9, 19
  power positions in, 27
  provincial, 8, 129
  Scottish, 96–7
  tutorial systems of, 96–8
University Council, the, 128
University Grants Committee, 8, 128–9
University of Liverpool, 129
University of London, 121, 129
University of London Institute of Education, 7
University of Oxford, 11, 94 ff., 121
University of Warwick, 128
university teachers, attitudes of, 130–1
Uppingham, 100
ushers, 90, 98–100

value-changes, 16–17
Vauxhall Motors Ltd, 64

'visibility', 55-6
vocational relevance, 19

Wakeford, J., 23, 24, 25, 122, 136
Wankowski, J. A., 18
Weaver Report, 76
Weber, Max, 3, 62, 79, 88-9
Welsford, E., 47
Westminster, 60, 98
Whyte, H., 105
Williams, D., 92
Wilson, James, 101

Winchester
    classroom planning, 56-7
    compulsory games at, 139
    George Moberly as headmaster, 81
    growth of, 59
    headmaster's income, 98, 102
Wiseman, S., 16
Wolverhampton Grammar School, 60
Woodhouse Grove, 83-4
Woodward, J., 79, 142
Wright Mills, C., 14

Young, M. F. D., 7